MYSTICISM:
A GUIDE FOR THE PERPLEXED

Continuum *Guides for the Perplexed*

Continuum's *Guides for the Perplexed* are clear, concise and accessible introductions to thinkers, writers and subjects that students and readers can find especially challenging. Concentrating specifically on what it is that makes the subject difficult to grasp, these books explain and explore key themes and ideas, guiding the reader towards a thorough understanding of demanding material.

Guides for the Perplexed **available from Continuum:**

Calvin: A Guide for the Perplexed, Paul Helm
Christian Bioethics: A Guide for the Perplexed, Agneta Sutton
Christology: A Guide for the Perplexed, Alan Spence
De Lubac: A Guide for the Perplexed, David Grumett
Kierkegaard: A Guide for the Perplexed, Clare Carlisle
The Trinity: A Guide for the Perplexed, Paul M. Collins
Wesley: A Guide for the Perplexed, Jason E. Vickers

Forthcoming:

Mercia Eleade: A Guide for the Perplexed, Charles Long
Sufism: A Guide for the Perplexed, Elizabeth Sirriyeh

CONTENTS

INTRODUCTION

We live in a world which is apparently characterized by instability, uncertainty and risk. We have begun to recognize the vulnerability of the planet on which we exist, whether from climate change or from the limited energy resources remaining. Threats of violence appear to pervade society, and our great institutions are no longer invulnerable. At such times, people search for certainty, and perhaps naturally look for the solace of religion. Yet perhaps paradoxically, the mainstream religions of the world do not appear to have the attraction which they once did, and indeed are in some cases finding it difficult to attract members.

There are many possible reasons for this. The contemporary world is certainly characterized by the transmission of knowledge and ideas on an unprecedented scale, largely facilitated by the internet. The result of this is that people around the world are exposed to a far greater variety of ideas than during any previous historical era. The material attractions of a secular society compete with the appeal of the spiritual life. Within the world of religion, people are exposed to many different sects and cults, and new religious movements. They can in a sense, pick and choose from a supermarket of spiritual ideas. They no longer, as in previous times, have the restricted choice of the religion of their family, cultural group or nation.

This diversity of ideas to which we all have access is clearly a good thing in many ways, but the globalization of the distribution of knowledge has led to the globalization of the distribution of choice. In religious terms, even the tiniest and newest of religious movements can ensure that its ideas reach potential members via the internet. Such a situation probably explains the enormous growth in new religious movements, and the consequent challenge to the established religions. However, this very growth in new religions and new religious groupings provides also at the same time, a source of uncertainty. In a world of so many different faiths, people ask themselves whether all these faiths are equally good. They ask themselves whether one group, or perhaps more than one, have a greater degree of truth than the rest. Is the one to which they belong better than the others? A world in which there are so many different groups is a world which is still fragmented and uncertain. The remedy for a world which is fragmenting more and more, and showing more and more signs of diversity, is not yet more fragmentation. It is, by contrast, a feeling of unity or unification. This is very often what people are looking for.

In times of uncertainty, the possibility of union and unity, is perhaps more reassuring than ideas of diversity and difference. It may be that people are trying to find confidence and reassurance in the idea that they are linked to the rest of humanity, and that they are linked to the rest of the natural world on the planet. This idea of connection and linkage is central to mysticism. Moreover, people are seeking a sense of direction in the universe. There is little reassurance in the idea that the universe is a sequence of completely random and uncoordinated events. There is considerable reassurance in the idea that there is a spiritual force behind the universe; that when an event takes place in the natural world, another event follows which either supports or balances the initial event. In other words, there is the notion of order and rationality in the universe. It is true that there are unpleasant natural events such as earthquakes, forest fires or floods, which cause great damage. Generally however, nature is resourceful and adaptable, and takes a relatively short time to make amends for the destruction.

In fact it is inaccurate in a sense, to call these events 'unpleasant' because they have no intrinsic intent or purpose. An earthquake does not set out to be malevolent, and to cause as much damage as possible. It is of course, a completely rational event resulting from stress and imbalance in the earth's crust. Once the disequilibrium has to some extent balanced itself, there is a return to greater stability and equilibrium. It is reassuring that when an event happens in the universe, a sequence of events respond to help return to a form of balance and stability. The idea that there is a controlling force behind the universe, even a spiritual force, is a mystical idea.

For many of us, the idea that we are part of something greater, which is also a part of us in return, is a reassuring idea. It provides a sense of purpose and significance in life. Such a mystical idea has been with us for a long time in various forms and in various traditions. Yet there is a timelessness about such ideas. They appeal to human beings in all ages, including our contemporary computer-based, globalized society. This book explores these ideas in both historical periods and in the modern world, and tries to show their practical relevance in day-to-day life.

The first part of the book examines the concept of mysticism, and the extent to which it is possible to provide a definition of the phenomenon. It explores related concepts such as pantheism and non-dualism, and then moves on to discuss the methods used by mystics to extend further the boundaries of their own spiritual under-standing and experience. These methods range from meditation in its various forms to the use of yoga, martial arts or dance. Finally, this first part looks at the lifestyle of mystics, and explores the different ways in which mystics choose to lead their lives, and interrelate with the rest of humanity. Traditionally many mystics have adopted a wandering, ascetic lifestyle, but some have practised their religious disciplines within conventional society.

The second part of the book explores the significance of mysticism within the main world religions and traditions. It examines the par-ticularities of individual mystical approaches while at the same time providing comparisons between different traditions. Within each faith, case studies of celebrated mystics are provided, exploring their lives and teachings.

In the final part, there is an attempt to analyse the nature of the mystical goal. It is extremely difficult to define, describe or otherwise understand the spiritual goal to which mystics aspire. By its very nature this is a subjective experience, and according to many mystics, difficult, if not impossible, to describe in mere words. Nevertheless, an attempt is made through the imperfect medium of the written word, to say as much as we can about this ultimate mystical goal. There is finally a contrast between orthodox religious traditions in the world, and the nature of mystical discipline and experience.

Mysticism is one of the least understood aspects of spiritual experience. It is, in a sense, hidden from the regular religious practi-tioner – a sometimes mysterious and strange aspect of the religious life. Nevertheless, it has never failed to attract people through the centuries – those who had an unquenchable desire to push back as far as they could, the boundaries of the life of the spirit. If this book can illuminate all but briefly, some aspects of this spiritual search, then it will have achieved a purpose.

PART I

WHAT IS MYSTICISM?

CHAPTER 1

THE CONCEPT OF MYSTICISM

SUMMARY

This chapter discusses the nature of mysticism and explores the main features of mystical experience. It analyses the concept of mysticism, and the extent to which it is difficult to define the term in a precise way. The chapter examines the connection between mysticism and such ideas as monism and pantheism. Finally, the chapter provides you with a concise summary of the key features of the mystical experience, and the way in which these relate to more traditional forms of religious practice.

INTRODUCTION

The main religious traditions of the world all share something in common. Since their inception they have developed patterns of religious activity which are relatively constant, and with which the majority of adherents comply. These forms of activity might include prayer, chanting, reading from scriptures or the practice of rituals. These are all mechanisms by which the members of the faith can try to achieve the goal of that faith. Generally speaking these practices also have a normative function – that is, they prescribe the kinds of activities which are expected of members, and which also help to define the membership of the religion. Clearly, religious practice varies from religion to religion, but there is usually a defined range of activity which is perceived as acceptable.

Mysticism, however, tends to step outside these normative boundaries. Those who might be described as mystics tend to seek a more direct and personalized religious experience, which is perhaps not as constrained as the orthodox tradition. In the case of theistic traditions, they may try to gain a direct subjective experience of God, or perhaps a sense of merging or unification with the Divine. In non-theistic traditions mystics may conceive of their spirituality rather differently. They may think of themselves as being in close communion with a spiritual or creative force which pervades the universe.

It is not easy to construct a short, precise definition of mysticism. A similar problem exists with trying to define the concept 'religion'. As you try to produce a definition with sufficient generality to include all the main world faiths, you realize your definition is so wide that it includes many other ideas as well. An alternative to trying to write a definition of mysticism, is to examine some of the ideas associated with the concept. In this way we begin to appreciate something of the range of the term. Ninian Smart, for example, wrote of a 'direct access to the divine' (1999: 209), and in doing so indicated one of the central elements in mysticism, that of an immediate and closely personal contact with God.

Although mystics may be a member of an orthodox religious tradition, and participate in the accepted practices, they typically do more besides. They develop spiritual strategies which help them in achieving this direct apprehension, in a way which, it is assumed, more traditional practitioners find difficult. The immediacy of this direct contact with God may be evident in a variety of ways, but it is generally agreed that one of the enduring aspects of the mystical experience is that it is very difficult to describe 'using normal vocabulary' (Cole, 2004: 51).

Everyday language is perfectly suitable for describing many aspects of the religious life. We can describe the appearance of a cathedral, a mosque or a temple using normal language, and equally we can write about what we observe of a religious ritual. The reason for this is that these are empirical objects which we can understand using our senses of sight, hearing and touch. If however, we seek to describe a person's intimate contact with the Divine, then to some extent we are moving outside the empirical realm. The person themselves may find it difficult to select appropriate terms to describe a very complex feeling, and we may equally find it difficult to understand, as we may not have had an analogous experience. The function of normal, empirical language breaks down because we are moving into what we might term a highly subjective, or perhaps phenomenological realm.

Not only may the mystic have difficulty in finding appropriate language to convey such spiritual experiences, but people in general may have difficulty in understanding the personal priorities of the mystic. In mysticism, there tends to be less emphasis on the practical matters of everyday life, and a concern with achieving a comprehension of the universe on a different plane. To gain this understanding, mystics may have a sense of surrendering themselves to God, or submitting themselves to a universal spiritual force. They attempt to achieve what Underhill (1999: 10) terms 'a total self-donation'.

In the world of everyday experience we tend to try to control the empirical world. Although we sense that the physical world is always changing, and is ultimately moving towards fragmentation and dissipation, we nevertheless struggle endlessly to limit that change and fragmentation. We know intellectually that the world is impermanent, but we strive to give our world the appearance of permanence. No amount of washing and polishing our cars will stop the onset of rust! Our wonderful new car is ultimately destined to be crushed and melted down! Now even if a mystic possessed a new car, he or she would not be concerned with its preservation. Mystics would not measure their lives through success or failure in preserving material possessions; rather they would evaluate their existence in terms of the spiritual plane. They would hope to gain an understanding and sense of union with a spiritual entity, and in seeking to achieve this would give of themselves wholeheartedly to that spiritual force.

Mysticism is also a term which is not used exclusively in a religious sense. People may refer to a 'mystical experience' when thinking of an event in the secular realm. For example, standing on a cliff top on a summer's day, staring out at the sea, may produce in us feelings of peace and tranquillity, and of a sense of oneness with the world. We may have similar experiences when walking in a beautiful natural setting, or perhaps when listening to music. Of course it depends on how we define 'religion', whether or not such experiences are included within our idea of religious experience. Parrinder (1995: 4) writes of 'transcendental experiences' in this context. There are occasions, often when we least expect them, when we feel transported out of the ordinary, into a rather special state, one no doubt which is difficult to define, but nevertheless very real and meaningful.

It is perhaps understandable that individuals who have such experiences, whether in the religious or secular spheres, wish to find a way to repeat them. Such experiences may be so meaningful that to leave their occurrence to serendipity may seem rather unsatisfactory. The obvious solution is to embark on a programme of spiritual or mystical training under the tuition of an experienced guide or *guru*, and this has indeed been part of the lives of mystics through the ages. Sheldrake (2007: 44) notes that in the early years of a developing monasticism in Egypt, it was the normal practice for a religious aspirant to live near to an older and more experienced spiritual teacher.

The function of the spiritual guide has traditionally been viewed as very important in mysticism. Within the communities of *sadhus* or wandering ascetics in India, it is typical for a young man in his early teens or younger, to be adopted as a disciple to an experienced teacher, and to serve a long term as a spiritual apprentice. Over a period of a number of years the disciple will receive tuition in meditation, Hindu scriptures and yogic practices, eventually becoming sufficiently experienced to take on his own disciples. There is a sense in which there is a spiritual lineage or succession, with mystical knowledge passing on through the generations. An analogous example might be found in Zen Buddhism, where monks receive tuition in *zazen* or meditation practice in a very disciplined environment. The head of the monastery passes on the tuition to the monks or nuns, who in turn pass it on to the next generation. It is considered by many practitioners that such a lineage may reasonably be viewed as stretching back to the Buddha himself.

Once we start to compare mystical practice or experience within different religious cultures, the question almost inevitably arises whether there is a kind of common core of experience throughout all religions. Such an idea would suggest that all mystics, from whichever tradition, share some experiences and ways of looking at the world, which at the same time, both unite them and distinguish them from more orthodox devotees of the world's faiths. Such a universalism (see Chryssides and Geaves, 2007: 361) of mystical experience might suggest a way of linking all world faiths, and of uniting certain spiritual practitioners.

Such an attempt would however be predicated upon establishing a precise definition of mysticism as a category. It would be necessary to separate clearly mystics from more traditional practitioners, and to find a means of delineating their differing spiritual experiences. Furthermore, it would be necessary to control for the effects of cultural factors which appear to engender a particular type of experience within one faith but not in another. The diversity of mystical experience suggests that this would be no easy task.

It is also argued that there are some specific religious or mystical experiences (Flood, 1999: 171–2) which are so much a part of a particular religious tradition, that it would be difficult to conceive of them in any other context. It may be, for example, that the practice and experience of repeating the name of God within the Sikh religion, while possessing some features of a similar practice in other faiths, is sufficiently distinct that we must consider it to all intents and purposes as a unique experience. The specific history, scriptural and theological context of Sikhism, it could be argued, creates such a particular cultural setting, that the repetition of God's name in that settings becomes a particularly Sikh experience.

MYSTICISM AND SPIRITUALITY

Mysticism as a concept also overlaps other religious concepts such as spirituality. It can be argued that the latter term is gradually being used more and more in settings which are not connected specifically with a particular religion (see Geaves, 2006: 98). One might extend this argument to mysticism also. It may be becoming legitimate to use the term mysticism to apply to experiences other than a sense of union with a divine being or with a form of universal spiritual force. The increasingly frequent use of meditation techniques and of yoga in secular settings, further emphasizes the rather fluid and evolving nature of contemporary religious experience.

The broadening use of the term mysticism does make it more and more difficult to distinguish a 'mystical' experience from the experiences of the larger membership of world faiths. It could be problematic to consider the mystical experience as being in someway 'special' or at a higher level of experience to the religious perceptions of others. To do so could be considered as a form of condescension, and the grounds for making this assumption might appear less than clear. Much here depends upon the way in which we define the boundaries of mysticism and of mystical experience. Furthermore there is the important question of whether it is possible to affirm the validity of mystical experience, and if so, in what way might we establish criteria for such an affirmation.

Our evidence of mystical experience depends very much upon personal, subjective accounts. People describe their experiences, often inevitably using language with which it is somewhat difficult to represent the intensity or profundity of the experience. There is much less evidence of mystical experience, from observers watching others having such experience. How then might we go about the task of attaching some validity to the experience?

On the one hand, we might compare the account of the mystical experience with accounts by other mystics. Finding points of similarity may point to a degree of validity. On the other hand, there is no reason why someone should not be replicating, either consciously or unconsciously, elements of previous accounts. A further possible criterion noted by Alston (2005: 216) is whether the person demonstrates such features of personality and behaviour which might be consonant with having mystical experiences. Such characteristics might include a sense of calmness and equanimity, or the exuding of a deeply religious approach to life. Again a person may exhibit these personality features entirely independently of having mystical experiences, and they would not constitute a positive affirmation. In short, it is difficult to establish the authenticity of mystical experience, although the kind of criteria suggested above do indicate degrees of validity.

The mystical experience has traditionally been associated with the general practice of withdrawing from the world. It has been felt by many mystics that living in the everyday world was not conducive to gaining spiritual insights, and to achieving their particular goal as a mystic. Some withdrew into monasteries, others adopted a solitary, wandering lifestyle, while others lived in caves, forests or the desert. Linked also to the idea of withdrawal from the world, was the adoption of an ascetic lifestyle. Mystics would perhaps typically only retain the barest of material possessions, and would consume only the minimum nourishment necessary to sustain life. The Jains of India are particularly noted for their ascetic traditions, and the historical Buddha famously adopted ascetic practices in an early attempt to reach an enlightened state.

One of the justifications for a lifestyle of withdrawal from the world lies in the apparently paradoxical idea of non-attachment to God or to any other object of mystical contemplation. It is an element in all the religions originating in the Indian subcontinent, and to perhaps a lesser extent in others, that the individual who aspires to true spirituality should eschew a sense of desire for things. 'Desire' may include certainly a wish to possess material possessions, but also, perhaps even more strongly, a desire to achieve a particular spiritual goal. The very act of wanting to gain or achieve something actually makes it infinitely more difficult to do so. This general principle appears to have been adopted by many mystical traditions.

The Zen Buddhist, for example, who wants to attain *satori* or enlightenment very badly, and whose entire meditation practice is controlled by a kind of spiritual obsession to achieve enlightenment, will simply not be in an appropriate psychological state to make progress. The mental state to cultivate is one of 'letting go', or abandonment of desires, to free the mind to make progress. In other words, by letting go of a wish for something, we attain it; by relinquishing our need for something, we gain it. There is an apparent paradox here, but upon reflection the principle of abandoning desires begins to make perfect sense.

Different religious and mystical traditions seem to have interpreted this principle in rather different ways, but the fundamental idea is at the basis of practices such as fasting or managing on the bare minimum of food to maintain reasonable health and vigour. While this idea of renouncing material pleasures such as delicious food is common in many mystical traditions, it also contains its own paradox. The mystic can become attached to the very principle of non-attachment! In other words, the mystic can become so obsessed with the principle of managing without food, that this becomes an end in itself. The mystic forgets that the fasting is simply a strategy towards a higher goal. Finally, some writers (Charlesworth, 2002: 166) have noted the apparent contradiction, that those who would have a close experience of God, should in fact, not become attached to this idea. In this way they are more likely to achieve it.

Not all religions or traditions have however advocated an ascetic approach to the mystical quest. The Sikh religion has always advocated that Sikhs should live an active role as part of society, as well as maintaining a spiritual approach to life. The two were not viewed as incompatible. The key principles of the faith were to be employed to help the individual live a moral and religious life, in the midst of the usual tensions and pressures of normal life. As Sikhism can ultimately be considered as a mystical religion, this can be thought of as a recommendation to live a mystical existence in the everyday world. This is much the same position as adopted by the theologian Teilhard de Chardin (see King, 1980: 212).

Mystical experience may be classified into experiences which are on the one hand external to the person, and on the other hand, those that are within the mind, and are independent of sensory experience. An example of the former might be if someone were hiking in the mountains and developed feeling of awe or even ecstasy, when confronted with the magnitude of the mountains and the breadth of the scenery. This might be conceptualized as feelings about God, or simply about the magnificence of nature. However, whatever the specific nature of the experiences, they are initiated by external stimuli, and hence this type of mystical experience is often termed extrovertive mysticism.

However, there are arguably types of mystical feeling which are perhaps independent of empirical experience. These might be said to include experiences during meditational practice, in which a feeling of bliss arises. Such a feeling is not caused to arise by a specific stimulus, and hence might be referred to as introvertive mysticism. The existence of *a priori* experiences, or those which are said to occur before and independent of empirical events is a problematic assertion, but at least this division does provide a way of thinking about mystical experience.

We have thus explored some of the different facets of mysticism, without attempting a precise definition. We will however return at the end of this chapter to the task of providing a rather more concise statement of the phenomenon. In the meantime, perhaps we can explore some related terminology, which again sheds some light on mysticism.

MONISM, PANTHEISM AND PANENTHEISM

There are a variety of interrelated terms which are used in religious studies, and which overlap to some extent with the idea of mysticism. Perhaps the most general term is 'monism'. This is the assertion or belief that the entire universe is interconnected in such a way that it is fundamentally impossible to distinguish the parts. In other words, the most accurate way to think of the universe is that it is basically a single entity. On one level this assertion seems to defy common sense, since people are all slightly different, and then again there are many different species of other animals and plants. Monism, however, is not considering this superficial differentiation of the universe, but the concept is rather suggesting that this diversity is linked together by a single spiritual force or entity, such that the universe is fundamentally unified. We may think of this spiritual force as God if we wish, but it may alternatively simply be a spiritual link which is not identified with a deity.

If we conceive of monism as referring to a single God, then that God will exist both externally to us in some transcendent realm, and also within us as an imminent deity. The fundamental characteristic of God, however, will be the idea of unity. If a mystic then, thinks of the universe in this way, then the task is to realize and understand this sense of unity in a fundamental, experiential way. Mystics need to fully comprehend that they are part of God, and God is part of them. They need to appreciate this, not in an abstract, intellectual manner, but to try to experience this on an emotional level. In this way they will truly understand the concept, rather than simply being taught it in an intellectual way.

A concept which is related to monism is that of pantheism. As the name suggests, this concept involves the idea that God is present throughout the universe. Perhaps more than that the concept also implies that God is part of everything in the universe, and everything is an element in God. We might go even further, and say that it is not possible to differentiate between God and the rest of the universe. If one subscribes to the view of pantheism, then one is logically also a monist. However, it is possible to be an advocate of monism while not accepting pantheism, simply because the monist does not need necessarily to subscribe to the concept of a God.

Pantheism is thus relevant to mysticism in the context of a mystic who is a member of a monotheistic faith. In that case the mystic may accept the proposition that the soul of the individual human being has within it an element of the Divine, and conversely the individual soul is also part of the Divine. The goal of the mystic then becomes the task of transforming this logical acceptance of a proposition into an experiential understanding. The pathway to that experience then relies upon the various strategies traditionally adopted by mystics, including prayer, contemplation and meditation.

A subtly different concept is that of panentheism. Like pantheism, it accepts the philosophical position that God is present in, and a part of the entire empirical universe. It does, however, attach rather more significance to God, in that the latter is viewed as greater and more important than the rest of the universe. God is perceived as certainly imminent, but also transcendent and all-powerful, and embracing the entire universe. Such a concept of God will tend to suggest worship and devotional practices on the part of the mystic, who offers the individual soul to the greater transcendent deity.

A further term which is in fairly frequent use, and which is connected with Hindu philosophy, is non-dualism. This is the philosophy that a concept of the world as two polar opposites is largely a failure. A dualistic philosophy would be one which, for example, recognizes the classical distinction between subject and object. Hence, a human being (the subject) looks at a pine forest (the object). Now in much mystical thinking there is the notion that the subject and object are not really separate. If mystics were looking at and contemplating the same forest, they would tend to regard themselves and the forest as a unity. Most mystics, even within a range of religious traditions, have to some extent regarded the existence of the individual ego as being of rather spurious validity. The reason for this is that in an attempt to achieve a sense of spiritual unity, they try to eliminate all sense of desire for the world. In this way the individual is free, and can more easily seek a close connection and understanding with God or an all-embracing entity. Therefore any way of life or thinking which seeks to emphasize a sense of opposites or duality in the world is the very antithesis of non-dualism. The latter idea is the philosophical basis of a number of Hindu schools of thought, and has been very influential over the years, with mystics.

EXOTERICISM AND ESOTERICISM

The adjectives exoteric and esoteric are used both in the context of religion, but also in everyday discourse. The word esoteric is probably the commonest in everyday language, carrying the suggestion of an area of knowledge which is rather unusual, obscure and difficult to understand. Exoteric on the other hand is used to signify something which is straightforward, commonly understood and available to the generality of individuals.

In terms of religion, exoteric knowledge or practice is that which is widely understood, and probably is part of regular festivals or ritual. It would apply to aspects of religious life which are for example, part of everyday worship. Esoteric knowledge or practice, however, would generally not be widely practised or understood. It might be confined to a minority of say, monastics, or it might require specialist skills to understand. It might for example, involve scriptures in an archaic language, expertise in which was limited to a few.

There are esoteric elements in all the major religions, and many of these are associated with mystical practice. There are also newer branches of religions or what might be termed new religious movements, which are largely esoteric, in the sense that there are relatively few members, and there is no particular attempt to spread the knowledge base of the group more widely. An example of a newer religious movement with strong mystical elements would be the Theosophical Society founded in 1875 by Helena Blavatsky. Its belief system could be described as monist, and it was much influenced by the Hindu religion. While never attaining a large membership, it has nevertheless been much discussed in spiritual and religious literature, and has retained a certain degree of influence in spiritually and mystically oriented circles.

It should be remembered of course that terms such as esoteric and exoteric do not necessarily reflect an element of reality in religious knowledge or experience. In employing such terms we are as human beings, trying to impose external categories on a subject about which it is usually very difficult to be precise. Such terms help us study and make sense of areas such as religion and mysticism, but we should not deceive ourselves, that they mirror reality in someway.

Much the same may be said of the concept 'mysticism' itself, and as Kripal (2006: 321–2) argues, mysticism is a relatively recent area of study. This is not to say that practices which we label as mystical have not been occurring in religions for many years. It is simply to remind ourselves that the act of grouping them together and regarding them as in someway related and interconnected is a more recent activity. Mysticism could be regarded, for example, as syncretistic. That is it draws together a number of different practices and beliefs from different faiths, and combines them under one heading. The scholarly activity of grouping activities and ideas together and giving them a name such as mysticism certainly makes the study of religion easier, but it is important that we are alert to the danger of reification. The latter is the act of apparently making something 'real' by, for example, applying a specialist term to it. Now this discussion is not intended to undermine the study of 'mysticism', but merely to pause and remind ourselves that it is an academic category created by human beings. What are 'real', are the many religious activities embraced within this term, and which have enormous significance for their practitioners.

MAIN FEATURES OF MYSTICISM

Mysticism is therefore a type of religious experience which involves a sense of union or merging with either God or an all-pervading spiritual force in the universe. There is perhaps an accompanying sense of the individual 'I' or ego being obliterated in this feeling of oneness with the Divine or with nature. There may be feelings of bliss or ecstasy, and the experience may be very difficult to describe in ordinary language. Mystics may have a guru to guide them on the spiritual path, and the mystic may practise various strategies such as yoga, meditation or contemplation. The mystic may live in a monastic community, or in fact live the life of a normal householder. As with many religious concepts it is difficult to provide a succinct definition, without excluding a number of activities which would be viewed as part of mysticism.

KEY IDEAS

All of the main religions of the world have elements of mysticism within their belief system. Mysticism is often slightly esoteric, or separated from the more orthodox teaching of the religion. Mystics themselves are also often considered to separate themselves from the world in one or more ways. They may become ascetics or mendicants, and may practice their teachings using methods which are considered slightly unusual. The ultimate goal is the union of the individual with either God, or with a spiritual force within the universe.

CHAPTER 2

APPROACHES USED BY MYSTICS

SUMMARY

This chapter examines the range of techniques used by mystics to achieve their goal. It explores the use of a variety of meditation techniques, including mantra, yoga and chanting. Finally the chapter discusses the connections between mysticism and such practices as calligraphy, archery, dance and martial arts. Although some approaches and mystical techniques are more typical of some religions than others, the chapter indicates the comparability between methods used by mystics of all faiths.

INTRODUCTION

Mystics have traditionally employed a wide variety of methods to progress along their chosen spiritual path. These methods vary considerably depending upon the particular culture or religious tradition. Despite this variation of practice, we can perhaps discern certain very general features which are shared by these methods.

One of the main practices is to try to calm the mind, and to stop it wandering from one thought to another. If this is achieved to some degree, then the individual can focus attention much more effectively on the nature of the specific mystical training. Not only to achieve this calmness of mind, but also as a technique in its own right, the mystic tends to use repetitive actions or sounds. This might involve the counting of the breath, or of beads on a rosary. It might also include the chanting of religious sounds or phrases, or the repetition of certain physical postures as in Hatha yoga. In relation to the latter example, mystical training often does include the integration of mental and physical practice. An obvious example is yoga, but meditation itself is usually practised using certain postures. In addition, dance, as in certain Sufi traditions, or archery and flower arranging, as in Zen Buddhist culture, relate physical motion to the practice of contemplation and the generation of calm. All in all then, even though there are many cultural variations, we may be able to discern certain shared trends in these practices.

MEDITATION

Of all the methods employed by mystics, meditation is arguably the most widespread, and is certainly used in one form or another in all the main world religions. The first aim of meditation is usually to calm the mind. If we reflect on the nature of our mind at any moment, we will usually realize that it is susceptible to rapid changes of thought. In modern life we are continually affected by a range of external stimuli, whether these be conversation, noises from outside the house, smells or television. These trigger thoughts in our minds. At the same time, thoughts arise in our minds almost spontaneously. Sometimes, for no apparent reason, we may start to worry about something at work, or we may suddenly remember that we have not sent someone a birthday card. This flow of changing thoughts is not only quite fatiguing, but it also means that we cannot reflect upon spiritual matters. The first step for most mystics is to try to slow down this stream of thought, so that they can calmly reflect on God or another object of contemplation. The method adopted usually involves training the mind to focus on a single object, to prevent it from moving rapidly from one thought to another.

The commonest object chosen in a number of religions, but notably in Hinduism and Buddhism, is the act of breathing (Cole, 2005: 19). The mystic sits cross-legged in the lotus position, and focuses the mind on the steady inhalation and exhalation of the breath in the nostrils. The breathing process as an object of meditation has the distinct advantage that it is a repetitive process, which further helps in the calming of the mind. This type of practice enables the mystic to concentrate the mind, as a precursor to further meditation exercises. As a different strategy for calming and concentrating the mind, some practitioners, for example in Theravada Buddhism, use walking meditation.

In this method the practitioner marks out a meditation path of perhaps 20 paces or so, and walks calmly up and down this 'path', slowly and methodically. The walking meditation may be combined with other techniques such as awareness of the breath. Walking meditation is usually an opportunity to practise mindfulness. As human beings we tend not to be very good at concentrating on what we are doing. When running for a bus for example, we are very unlikely to be thinking about the act of running, but we are much more likely to be thinking about a job we have to do at work, or about who we will meet for lunch, or what we will do that evening. Walking meditation is an opportunity to be very mindful. The practitioner concentrates on the feeling of the sole of the foot being placed on the ground, and then the body's weight gradually shifting to the other foot as that is placed ahead. The mind concentrates on the feeling of the ground through the sole of the shoe. In places one can feel stones, while in other positions the earth feels smooth. The mind is conscious of the muscles of the leg, as they change tension during the rhythmic walking motion. The mind becomes calmer, and is conscious of many things not normally sensed. It is the difference between driving in a car down a country lane, and walking down a lane slowly. In the latter case one has the time to notice the variety of plants in the hedgerow, the bird song and the butterflies. It is a slower and calmer experience, but richer for all that.

Mindfulness is important because it helps mystics to focus upon the here and now. It is very easy to allow the mind to stray into becoming preoccupied with the future, or dwelling too much upon the past. It tends to be a characteristic of mystical techniques, that mystics try to concentrate upon the present. They try to cultivate a heightened awareness of even the most apparently trivial event in the present. They tend to think of the present as, in a sense, the only valid reality. By means of a mindful concentration on present events, they try to develop a more intense view of the world: both the physical world and the world of the spirit.

Meditation has always been an element in all world faiths, but perhaps more central to some than others. It was the central process used by the historical Buddha to achieve enlightenment, and since then has been used in various forms throughout the different schools of Buddhism. It has been a central assertion of Buddhism that it was not sufficient to study Buddhist precepts in a purely academic fashion. It was, on the contrary, necessary to use meditation techniques to gain an experiential appreciation of Buddhist principles, to make spiritual progress, and moreover, to attain enlightenment

(Armstrong, 2000: 96). Many other strategies have been integrated with meditation in different traditions, and one of the best known is the use of spiritual sounds or syllables.

A mantra is a religious syllable, sentence or group of sentences which is repeated as either a specific aid to meditation or to achieve spiritual or mystical insight. Sometimes the actual name of God in a specific culture or language may be used as a mantra. As a technique it is popular, perhaps partly because it is easy to use, and may be employed at any time of the day. Normally meditation involves finding a quiet, solitary place and ensuring one can remain undisturbed for a while. A mantra can however be employed in even the busiest and most stressful of situations. A mystic may be given a specific mantra by a spiritual teacher, or may decide to adopt one in particular. Once a mantra is either given by a guru, or selected by oneself, it is normal to retain that mantra and not to keep changing it.

Mantras have traditionally been used very widely in Hinduism, and of these the single syllable *Aum* is perhaps the most celebrated. This sound is intended to represent Brahman, the spiritual force behind the universe. *Ram* or *Rama*, one of the names representing God, is another popular mantra among Hindus. Some Hindu mantras have also passed in popular culture, perhaps the most celebrated example being the Hare Krishna mantra. Within Buddhism, mantras are perhaps more widely used in Tibetan traditions than in other schools, and the most celebrated mantra is probably *Om mani padme hum*. As Tibetan traditions of Buddhism are becoming more common in the West, this mantra is becoming relatively well known.

Mantras are also used in other Indian religions such as Sikhism. This is a religion which has a clear mystical goal. The ultimate religious purpose for each individual Sikh is to attain a form of mystical union with God, and to this end a number of different spiritual strategies and exercises are recommended. One of the most important of these involves a practice known as *nam simaran*, or the repetition and remembering of the name of God. The Sikh scripture, the Guru Granth Sahib, also begins with a celebrated mantra, the so-called Mul Mantra. The first three syllables of this, *Ek Omkar* (There is one God), are a clear statement of the monotheism which is at the heart of Sikh mysticism.

In many religious traditions, a form of counting is employed to ensure that the name of God or other mantra is repeated the requisite number of times. The original method of doing this would almost certainly have been to count on the fingers. In some Islamic traditions, and particularly in some Sufi orders, the practice of *dhikr*, or the repetition of the names of God, is assisted by the use of prayer beads or *misbaha*. Each of the latter usually contains 99 beads, each bead standing for a particular name of Allah.

In Christianity there is a long tradition of using methods of counting to support the saying of prayers and as an aid to meditation practices. In some traditions, monks would use strands of string or rope with appropriate numbers of knots tied in them. In others beads or other objects would be strung on a loop. Perhaps the best-known method is the use of the rosary within the Roman Catholic Church. The use of the rosary involves saying a series of prayers, including the Lord's Prayer, in repeated cycles a prescribed number of times. Between the sections of repeated prayers, there is often a period of meditation upon Jesus Christ or the Virgin Mary. The arrangement of the beads on the rosary is such as to assist the individual in remembering the number of times the sequence has been repeated.

In Indian religions the word *mala* is used to describe a set of beads which are used in meditation for the purpose of counting repetitions of a mantra. *Japa* is the actual process of meditation in this fashion. In Hinduism a set of mala beads usually consists of 108 beads. The beads are often made from the seeds or wood of plants which are regarded as particularly holy or auspicious. The Tulsi plant is an example of this. During the use of mala beads the mantra can be said aloud during repetition, or it can be spoken silently under the breath. The overall purpose with all of these different methods of using prayer beads in different religions is to release the meditator from the task of remembering the number of repetitions of the mantra. In this way the individual can concentrate on the spiritual aspect of the meditation.

Some particular approaches to meditation have been developed in Japan, originally adapted from teachings transmitted from China. These variants of meditation are part of the Zen Buddhist tradition. The aspirant who wished to join a Zen Buddhist monastery in Japan, traditionally found it very difficult to be admitted. The initial response would be to tell the would-be monk that there was no room for an additional person in the monastery. The aspirant was then expected to wait outside the main gate of the monastery for perhaps 24 hours, before again seeking admission. The response was likely to be the same. If the postulant was sufficiently persistent, then eventually it was likely they would be allowed entry. The whole process was designed to test commitment to the training, and certainly commitment was a quality much needed in someone seeking to embark on training within the Zen tradition. Life in the monastery consisted of long periods of hard physical work, which were perceived as very much an element of the Zen training, along with substantial periods of *zazen* or Zen meditation.

The Rinzai School of Zen is famous for its use of the *koan* in meditation practice. After a period of practice in concentration meditation, the Zen master allocates the novice a specific verbal puzzle for reflection. These koans are designed in order not to be susceptible to rational and logical analysis. A particularly celebrated koan is for example, 'What is the sound of one hand clapping?' The novice is expected to reflect upon this puzzle during periods of meditation. At fairly extended intervals the novice has a brief interview with the Zen master, and is expected to explain or respond in someway to the koan which has been given. Clearly a logical response in terms of actually describing the sound of one hand is quite impossible. However, the purpose of the exercise is that the student should be able to demonstrate in someway, that progress has been made in terms of the goals of Buddhist practice. There is no specific 'right answer' to a koan, otherwise students would quickly learn these! The master will accept an answer, if it seems appropriate to the particular individual and to the context. The Soto School of Zen Buddhism, however, uses a different approach to meditation. Observation of the breath is employed as a means of developing a tranquil mind and encouraging concentration. Meditation involves simply sitting and observing the activity of the mind, with the coming and going of thoughts.

A further strategy employed in some mystical traditions employs the use of designs and diagrams known as *mandalas* or *yantras*. These are often symmetrical coloured patterns with extremely complex designs. They may be made in a variety of materials. Some are permanent in that they are painted on paper or canvas, while others are impermanent in structure, being made through the careful positioning of coloured sand. The latter practice occurs among Tibetan Buddhists and also traditionally among some indigenous North American tribes. The mandala is often perceived as a visual representation of the spiritual nature of the universe and as such, is sometimes used as the object of meditation or of other mystical practices.

Within some Hindu traditions the yantra is an element of esoteric practices associated with Tantric Yoga.

YOGA

The term yoga derives from a Sanskrit word meaning 'to yolk together', and one interpretation of this is that it refers to the mystical joining or union of the individual soul with the cosmic soul or Brahman. There are many different schools of yoga, each devoted to a different practice, although *Hatha yoga*, or the yoga associated with physical postures, has become the most widely known in the West. Some of the mystical techniques, such as the use of mantra such as Aum, are very much a part of yoga.

One way of conceptualizing yoga is that within classical Hinduism, it links a number of different religious beliefs and practices into a holistic system of spiritual and mystical practice. It can be argued that yoga is essentially mystical in nature since its ultimate goal is *moksha*, or release of the individual from *samsara*, the continual cycle of birth and rebirth. Liberation from samsara provides the opportunity of uniting with Brahman. This union of the individual soul with God suggests the mysticism inherent in yoga.

Hatha yoga typically involves a variety of breathing exercises known as *pranayama*, and a range of different physical postures, the *asanas*. The latter are much used in Hindu culture as a form of physical training, just as in the West, although in India, there is generally a greater awareness of their derivation from, and association with, spiritual training. The various kinds of sitting postures used in meditation are essentially asanas. Quite apart from the use of Hatha yoga by those with a religious inclination in India, the postures are much employed by the wandering Hindu ascetics known as *sadhus*. Such holy men and women integrate yoga postures into their daily discipline, and some will use a particular posture to extremes by holding it for many months or indeed years. Some sadhus view such austerities as an essential part of the mystical quest. Indeed, mystical practices are typically not restricted to merely mental activity. Physical activity, as we have seen with walking meditation, is perceived as an essential part of the spiritual search. In this way, mental training and physical training are combined in the ultimate spiritual quest. There are, however, many other mystical techniques, and some of these employ the use of what we may broadly describe as artistic activities.

MYSTICISM AND ART

Human beings seem always to have had a desire to produce artistic representations of religious ideas and events. By so doing, we have attempted to make the most complex concepts perhaps a little more real. The visual image has perhaps helped us to a better understanding of our respective faiths. These representations have of course differed greatly depending upon culture and religion, and have included calligraphy, painting and sculpture.

In about the twelfth and thirteenth centuries in China, a style of landscape painting developed which was very much influenced by the mystical thought of Taoism and Buddhism. The paintings were often created largely in monochrome or perhaps with a very limited palette. The subjects usually included sweeping mountain ranges, mists descending into steep valleys, narrow paths winding up precipitous rock faces, gushing torrents or waterfalls, bamboo groves or wind-blown pine trees clinging to mountain ledges. In other words, the paintings emphasized the scope and grandeur of nature. It was typical of such paintings that a great deal of the space of the painting was left blank, or perhaps occupied by vast expanses of sky and clouds. There was not the tendency evident in some Western art to fill in and use up every part of a canvas.

Yet the important element of these Taoist and Buddhist paintings was often very small and scarcely discernible in the painting. There might be a tiny figure of an old man, perhaps a monk, edging his way up a steep path along a valley, with only a stick to support him. He might be doubled-up against the wind, and clearly struggling against the elements. In the distance, far away above the snow-line, we might just see the roof of a small monastery, presumably his destination. In other paintings, in the valley bottom, alongside a river and perhaps set in a grove of bamboo we will see a tiny, humble hut, and sitting cross-legged in the doorway is a monk meditating. Behind him, rising up from the valley floor, are vast, ominous mountain ranges.

All of this is of course highly symbolic. The use of empty space in the paintings can be seen as a representation of the mind during meditation. The mystic tries, during meditation, to empty the mind of all desires, to expect nothing, to abandon the wish that the world be a certain kind of place. There is an attempt to cultivate non-attachment. This sense of calming and emptying the mind is common to many mystic traditions, but is represented in these paintings by the use of space.

The relation of man to nature is also reflected in the paintings. The natural world is held in great esteem in both Chinese and Japanese religious traditions. Mystics try to retire to a peaceful, natural location to meditate. However, apart from indicating the tranquillity of nature, the paintings are also comparing the magnitude of the natural world in comparison with humanity. The human figure seems lost within the enormous scope of the landscape, emphasizing the insignificance of humanity. In addition, the human figure is usually represented as a religious figure often meditating, or travelling to a remote monastery, as if on a pilgrimage. This style of painting was transmitted to Japan, where it also became a central form of expression of Zen Buddhism. The paintings fulfilled two functions. First, they were an object of contemplation, to help people reflect upon the nature of human beings within Taoist and Buddhist philosophies. Secondly, however, the actual creation of the paintings was also a spiritual exercise, and many of the artists were themselves monks, a celebrated example being the artist Sesshu.

There are many other forms of painting in other religions, which have a mystical element or purpose. In Christianity, and particularly in the Eastern Orthodox Church there is a long tradition of painting ornate images on for example, wooden blocks, to create *icons*. These paintings may represent Jesus Christ or the Virgin Mary, or perhaps be representations of saints. Icons serve a number of purposes, one of which is as part of contemplation or meditation practice. Within Hinduism, *murti* are visual representations of deities, which may consist of paintings or painted sculptures. They are again used as an object to aid meditation, or as part of *puja* ceremonies involving prayers and the making of offerings.

In Tibetan Buddhist culture, the religious paintings known as *thanka* are very much celebrated. They may be painted on cloth, canvas or paper, and are typically very colourful representations of *Mahayana* or *Vajrayana* deities, and images of the Buddha. Thanka are highly decorative, and use a large number of potential images and decorative themes, combining them differently in individual paintings. The structure of a *thanka* is highly organized and symmetrical, and is symbolic of Buddhist religious belief. The decorative themes, and the organization of the painting, are symbolic of various

Buddhist themes. Like icons they have a variety of functions, but are used as an aid to meditation.

Calligraphy is also very significant in some religious and mystical traditions. The Tibetan script is used to write mantras on Buddhist prayer wheels, which are rotated as part of spiritual practice. In Islam, calligraphy has a particular significance, since it is used to replicate either parts or all of the Qur'an. There are a number of different styles of Arabic calligraphy, some of which are very ornate. Finally the ancient Siddham script was used to write out many of the early Tantric Buddhist manuscripts. In many cases religious calligraphy has acquired a significance over and above the functional purpose of recording prayers, mantra or scriptural texts.

LITERATURE AND DANCE

Besides painting and calligraphy, the mystical search has also been connected with other art forms. Poetry has been much used by mystics as an expression of their quest for the 'ultimate'. One example is the Japanese *haiku* tradition. The haiku is a brief poem which is written in a highly structured way, normally using about seventeen syllables to express a brief idea. It is very much linked to the Zen Buddhist tradition. Haiku usually describe aspects of nature such as snow collecting on bamboo, flowering cherry blossom, streams, falling leaves, the colours of the seasons and living things in their natural habitat. Superimposed on that, however, are aspects of human experience which reflect something of Zen philosophy. Haiku may reflect a number of themes such as the impermanence of life, or of a sense of tranquillity in a natural location. The writing of haiku may be regarded as a form of meditation, or indeed the poems themselves may be viewed as the objects of reflection. Haiku poets, such as Matsuo Basho (who died in 1694), were often very influenced by Zen philosophy. Basho himself spent much of his later life travelling throughout Japan in a very simple way, carrying very few possessions. He visited shrines and wrote travel journals which are still famous today. Within those journals he also wrote many haiku to express his feelings and to describe places he saw.

Dance is another means of artistic expression used by some mystics to try to achieve a sense of the Divine and a feeling of comprehending God directly. Particularly celebrated are some orders of Islamic mystics or *Sufis*. They are popularly known as Dervishes or 'whirling' Dervishes because of the spinning dance carried out wearing long gowns. The most famous Dervish order is perhaps the Mevlevi order which was established by those influenced by the Persian poet Rumi. The order has been historically based in Turkey. The whirling dance is a form of *dhikr*, or a means of remembering God. The dance is carried out in a very ritualized manner, and through it the mystic tries to reach higher and higher levels of understanding of God.

FURTHER TECHNIQUES

Mystics have used many other methods by which they have sought to attain a higher spiritual understanding. Some of these are perhaps less spiritual techniques in themselves, as practices which accompany the basic method of meditation. An example is the practice of archery in Japan. Like the writing of haiku, this practice reflects much of the spirit of Zen Buddhism. It can be regarded simply as a sport, but at a more sophisticated, philosophical level it exemplifies much of the principles of Buddhism. Known as *kyudo* in Japan, it is governed traditionally by a range of rituals in terms of the drawing and firing of the bow. The ultimate aim is to create a situation where the bow, the archer and the target constitute a form of spiritual whole. In a strange and apparent contradiction in terms, the archer does not actively try to hit the target, but by concentrating upon the drawing and release of the bow leaves the arrow to find its own way to the target. We can think of this as perhaps an example of the Buddhist principle of non-attachment. Paradoxically, if the archer tries too hard to hit the target, then he may fail to do so. However, by concentrating upon the process rather than the result, he will achieve his goal. Such is broadly the philosophy of kyudo.

The principle of not becoming obsessed with achieving goals seems to be a recurring theme of mystics. It is found, for example, in the Bhagavad Gita, where there is the emphasis upon devoting one's actions to God, rather than acting out of a desire to achieve something. It is part of the apparent contradiction of this philosophy that when one tries not to become too focused on the achievement of goals, sometimes one achieves those very goals. This is not to say that one should not have goals in life, or try to achieve something, but rather that one should not be too attached to those goals. Nor is this a philosophy of quietism or of withdrawal from any sense of trying hard to do something. It is making a subtle distinction between on the one hand the state of mind of working very hard at something and being very concerned about achieving the end, and on the other hand of working just as hard, but of finally letting things take their own course.

The same principle applies in a way with the integration of Buddhism with martial arts practice. When Buddhist teachings were brought by monks, including Bodhidharma, to China in the fifth and sixth centuries CE, monasteries were gradually established to act as both repositories of scriptural texts and as places of meditation and teaching. One of these monasteries was the Shaolin monastery in Hunan province, later to become very celebrated as a place of Kung Fu tuition. On one level it seems paradoxical that Buddhism, a way of life which is very much associated with peace and non-violence, should in any way be associated with martial arts. Indeed it is hard to know for certain how and why martial arts became established within the parameters of some Buddhist traditions. One hypothesis is that the monks and nuns needed to protect themselves from aggressors, and needed a form of self-defence which to some extent could turn the violence of the aggressor back against themselves. It certainly seems that at the heart of the different approaches to martial arts is a sense of the importance of defence rather than aggression. In addition, the discipline and repetition required in the training, may well have served as a form of meditation.

It is worth mentioning briefly two other features of mystical practice in some traditions. In Hinduism and also in Tantric Buddhism we find the tradition of using hand gestures or *mudra*, which carry a ritual significance. These gestures are evident in dance and in Buddhist sculptures. A well-known example of mudra is the way in which the hands are positioned during meditation. There are slightly different customs for this in different religions, and in different schools within religions, and each gesture usually has a particular significance.

Ritual is important in mystical practice just as it is in any other form of religious practice. In *ikebana* or Japanese flower arranging we see an activity which is on one level an art form and an aesthetic, yet which at the same time is influenced by the principles of Zen. The flower arrangements are never ornate, but restricted to very simple compositions using a small number of flowers. The way in which the flowers are arranged normally adheres to certain principles of

asymmetry, and the act of placing flowers in a harmonious orientation is itself a type of meditation.

We can thus see that in different cultures and religions, a wide
range of different customs and activities have been incorporated into
what we might term mystical practice, but that they all embrace some
common features.

KEY IDEAS

At the heart of mystical practices is meditation. This may take a
variety of different forms but the central idea is to calm the mind,
and hence to enable the individual to concentrate on an analysis
and understanding of the human condition. Depending upon the
tradition, this may also involve a sense of union with the Divine, or a
feeling of reaching a supreme or enlightened state of consciousness.
The practice of the mystic is also one of 'letting go' of the phenome-
nal world, and of trying to be unattached to many of the features
of material existence. Whether practice involves the use of physical
activity, prayer beads or participation in aesthetic activity, there
remains an emphasis upon trying to relinquish a sense of the self or
of the ego.

CHAPTER 3

LIFESTYLES OF MYSTICS

SUMMARY

This chapter explores the kinds of lifestyle normally associated with mystics. It examines the monastic tradition in different faiths, and also the lifestyle of the ascetic or solitary hermit. The chapter discusses some of the practices associated with mystics such as fasting and abstinence from many of the material pleasures of everyday life. Although the mystic is normally perceived as living a life removed from that of society, there are also examples of individuals who seem to have been able to combine the secular and the mystical life. The chapter will explore this phenomenon, and also evaluate the question of whether it is necessary to have a teacher or guru to acquire and develop mystical knowledge.

INTRODUCTION

We do tend to have a preordained image of the mystic and of the life which they lead. This image probably derives in part from the real lives of mystics, and perhaps partly *a priori* from our theoretical concept of the mystic. Perhaps we can start by trying to construct a general picture or 'ideal type' of the lifestyle of the mystic, and then apply this to real situations within a range of different religions.

Traditionally, the mystic is generally perceived as someone who lives apart from the mainstream of society. This may involve living in an extremely remote place, or perhaps simply living slightly removed from society on the outskirts of a village or town. This may be because some mystics maintain an interaction with ordinary people, having a role involving teaching or giving spiritual advice. Other mystics may, however, live a wandering lifestyle, with no fixed place to live. We also normally think of mystics as having a fairly basic lifestyle, or perhaps being rather ascetic in their way of life. They are usually conceived as living in a cave or a simple hut, with very few possessions. If they lead a wandering lifestyle, then they may only possess what they can carry. The rationale for this is the assumption that too many worldly possessions obstruct the spiritual quest, and divert the mystic's attention from a concern for God to a concern for the security of material possessions.

This very basic material existence is usually linked in our imagination with the mystic having very frugal meals, perhaps composed of simple vegetarian food. The rationale again is the assumption that eating rich and delicious food distracts the attention of the mystic from the goal of spiritual union with God. Spiritual progress is also associated in many religions with the idea of renunciation, and of giving up something pleasant for a period of time. Mystics are simply thought of as taking this one step further, and renouncing things more or less permanently. There is also the general idea that mystics will have few attachments in the world. Mystics are generally thought of as unmarried and maintaining a celibate lifestyle. They may not have any personal money, although they may provide advice on the spending of communal funds, for example, in a monastery. Again, if a mystic were to be concerned for the welfare of spouse or children, it is assumed that this would provide a digression from the spiritual route which has been undertaken.

Sometimes the mystic is conceived as a kind of exemplar of the spiritual life, someone who can inspire and motivate ordinary people. The latter perhaps see in the mystic the noble ideals of life, and view the mystic as a form of inspiration. There is thus often a kind of symbiotic relationship between lay people and the mystic. People, on the one hand, give alms to the mystic, perhaps in the form of food, or other necessary physical needs, while the mystic, on the other hand, provides spiritual advice. Equally well, the mystic sometimes receives mystical advice from others. It is often the case that mystics are part of a spiritual 'line', receiving initiation and teaching from older, more experienced mystics, and subsequently passing on their own wisdom to young, aspiring seekers.

Finally, we may have the concept of the mystic as being involved in practices which are a little mysterious. Mystics perhaps have the reputation of being involved in unusual practices, of having access to rather esoteric knowledge or understanding, excluded from ordinary people. They may be thought of as repositories of secret knowledge, which is comprehensible only to the initiated.

This is therefore an outline sketch of how some people may view mystics. Let us explore now how this generalized view is reflected within the reality of religious traditions.

THE SOLITARY QUEST

The idea of seeking God on one's own in a quiet, secluded place, is one of the abiding images of the mystic. One of the earliest documented examples in the Christian tradition is that of Saint Anthony in third-century Egypt. Devoted to the religious life from a very young age, he withdrew into the desert to live in solitude for many years. Although he later founded a monastery, he is remembered principally for his solitary search for spiritual enlightenment in the desert. The life of the hermit was motivated partly by a sense of replicating the time Jesus spent in the wilderness, and the belief that the way to find God must involve the solitary struggle of the individual person with the internal trials and tensions of the human soul. Many of the hermits who lived in the Egyptian desert at this time were not truly solitary, since some lived relatively close to others, or younger disciples would move to live in proximity with their teachers. Very often these informal groupings led later to the establishment of monasteries. Even when the monastic tradition became very well established in Europe during the twelfth century, there still existed the tradition of the isolated hermit devoted to a solitary life of introspection.

The idea of withdrawing from the world to lead the life of a mystic is very much embedded in the Hindu religion. In fact, within the classical Vedic system, there is the concept of viewing life as consisting of four main stages. The first stage is that of the Brahmacharya. This is the first period of a person's life lasting for 20 or 25 years. During this time the person is a student, receiving religious training, and perhaps being under the guidance of a guru. The second stage of life is that of Grihastha, or the period of earning a living, being a parent, and rearing children. After about the age of 50, the person gradually begins to withdraw from an occupation in the material world, and devotes themselves more and more to spiritual pursuits. This stage is known as Vanaprastha. Finally, there is the stage of the

Sannyasin, where people cut themselves off from everyday life, and withdraw into the forest or mountains, to live the life of a hermit. There they meditate and reflect upon God, until they leave this world. Their goal at this stage is moksha, or release from the endless cycle of birth and death.

One of the most celebrated instances of withdrawal from the world is that of Siddhartha Gautama, the man who became the Buddha. After he had left his father's palace in search of an ultimate spiritual understanding, he tried a variety of methods of meditation and yoga. Finally he tried the life of a solitary ascetic depriving himself of food. He almost died of malnourishment, but was rescued by a girl who fed him a small amount of rice and milk.

Another historical example of withdrawal from everyday life is that of Bodhidharma, the monk who is reputed to have brought Buddhist teachings to China. At one stage, eager to make spiritual progress he went to live in a cave, and spent nine years staring at a wall in meditation. Milarepa, the eleventh-century Tibetan mystic, also famously lived and meditated in a cave for many years.

In more recent times, there are a number of accounts of meditators abandoning the comforts of modern life, for the hardships of an ascetic existence. Mackenzie (1998) describes the life of Tenzin Palmo, a Western Buddhist nun, who meditated for many years in a cave in the Himalayas. In a similar vein, Ajahn Chah (2005) the Thai Buddhist meditation teacher, describes the hardships undergone by monks and nuns at his monastery in Thailand.

FASTING

Self-denial, particularly in terms of food, is practised in many different religious traditions. Jains are normally vegetarian and also practice fasting on a regular basis. An extreme version of this practice is that of fasting to death. When some Jain monks are reaching old age and feel that they may not have long to live, they may commence a long fast until death. They regard this as a profound mystical experience.

Buddhists generally do not fast, since going without food for a protracted period of time would be viewed as contrary to the Buddha's teaching of the Middle Way. In other words it would be rather too extreme. Nevertheless, within the Theravada tradition, monks and nuns are extremely abstemious in terms of food. In a typical pattern for the monastic day, they will rise in the early hours, and after a period of meditation and chanting will eat breakfast of tea and a bowl of gruel or rice. There may be some sugar to add to this, but it will be very simple fare. At noon they will eat the only meal of the day. In Buddhist countries this will depend on what is given to the monks and nuns during the alms round in the surrounding area. In Western countries, some food may be given by laity or bought by lay supporters from financial donations to the monastery. In any case, the food will be simple, the purpose being to sustain the health of the body, rather than to be attractive to the sense of taste. One of the purposes of Buddhist training is to develop a sense of non-attachment, and the eating of delicious food will encourage a sense of attachment to such pleasures. For the remainder of the day, the monks and nuns may not consume any nourishment. They may drink water, and are usually allowed to drink tea without milk or sugar. This is regarded as having no calorific value, and hence not breaking the fast. Sometimes, if a monk or nun is feeling unwell, the abbot of the monastery may permit an additional ration of food, such as some cheese.

The alms round and the sense that monks and nuns have to rely on others for food does provide some lessons for the Buddhist mystic. The Buddhist mendicant cannot simply desire some food, and go and buy it in the way which is possible for a layperson. The monk or nun is not permitted to handle money. This system is a continual reminder to Buddhists that they depend on others for their survival, and that human beings live as an interdependent community. Some days they may receive a reasonable amount of food from the alms round, while on other days they may receive little or none. This is a constant reminder that life is an impermanent phenomenon, and human beings cannot totally rely upon their having the means to sustain life.

Fasting as an aid to spiritual awareness is also a key element of the practices in Islam during the month of Ramadan. This is the holiest month of the Islamic calendar, and all Muslims, unless they are exempt for special reasons, should participate in the fast. The fast lasts for each day of the month from sunrise to sunset, and is certainly arduous, making great demands in terms of determination and motivation from Muslims. The month of Ramadan is also a time when Muslims are expected to be particularly careful and thoughtful in terms of acting in a spiritual manner, and thinking about Allah. The purpose of the actual fast is to help to take the mind away from material things, and to focus it upon the religious life. In particular, fasting is one of the practices which helps Muslims to remember God, and to aspire to the highest virtues of Islam. Sufis often participate in the practice of *dhikr*, which is the act of remembering or repeating the name of God. Fasting is sometimes seen as a practice which supports and relates to that of the remembering of God's name (Chittick, 2000). Muslims are also expected to fast for six days in the month following Ramadan.

Within the Christian tradition, the 40 days before Easter are celebrated as Lent, and historically associated with fasting. The 40 days are intended to represent the 40 days which Jesus spent in the wilderness being tempted by Satan. The customs of fasting have varied over the centuries, and vary now between different Christian churches. It may be more normal nowadays to relinquish a particular luxury, or element of the diet, for Lent. People may decide not to eat meat or eggs during Lent, or may choose some other item to give up. Whatever the detail of the observance, the general purpose, as in the above examples, is to concentrate the mind upon the religious life.

THE COMMUNAL LIFE AND THE SUPPORT OF THE SPIRITUAL GUIDE

Although mystics have often sought the solitary life, they have also developed the custom of living in some sort of community to provide mutual support. This varies from a few mystics living within walking distance of each other, to meet from time to time for discussion, to the idea of a closed monastic community. Communal life often also developed because religious aspirants would be attracted to a particular teacher, and they would gather near that person to receive spiritual advice and guidance. Sometimes the teacher would be a gifted individual who inspired disciples, while within some traditions there was a sense of spiritual succession. In other words, teachers could trace back their lineage through earlier teachers. The specific spiritual or mystical teaching was regarded as having been transmitted from generation to generation, from teacher to teacher.

The idea of a lineage of spiritual teachers is present in a number of religions. In Sikhism, for example, the spiritual leadership of the community started with Guru Nanak and was passed on through a series of nine further gurus, concluding with Guru Gobind Singh. Finally the Sikh scripture, the Guru Granth Sahib, was declared as the Guru. The teachings of Sikhism can be considered to have a mystical element, to the extent of the remembrance of the name of God, using the method of *nam simran*, and the ultimate goal of the achievement of a sense of unity with the Divine.

A further interesting example of the existence of a spiritual lineage is in Zen Buddhism. According to tradition, when the Buddha was teaching one day, he held up a flower to the assembled audience. No one understood the significance of this action, except for one monk who smiled at the Buddha. The latter realized that he had understood what he was trying to transmit. That teaching was then passed on through a series of teachers down the centuries, becoming the cornerstone of the Zen Buddhist tradition. This teaching has certain mystical elements in that it is transmitted in a very personal manner, from individual to individual, without recourse to scriptural texts. Even today, the Zen tradition relies very much upon practical activities, and notably sustained periods of meditation, under the careful tutelage of a monastery abbot or accepted Zen master. In other words one attains enlightenment in Zen, not through the careful study of scriptures, but through a gradual realization of what it means to be enlightened, partly through the observation of experienced practitioners and partly by means of one's own reflections.

Of all the world's religious traditions, it is perhaps in India that the idea of the spiritual teacher and disciple has the longest history. The sadhus or wandering mendicants of India, may in someways, appear to lead solitary and independent lives, but they are usually situated within clear religious traditions and have religious teachers. A sadhu will usually have had a guru from a young age, who will have provided guidance until such a time as the disciple was equipped to lead a more independent life. The sadhu will normally however, return to see his guru at certain times, which may be at special festivals or gatherings. Noted teachers may also establish and live in spiritual communities or ashrams, along with a fluctuating number of their disciples and lay people. The idea of the ashram has a long tradition in India. It may be a very modest and unpretentious establishment, or a substantial and internationally famous foundation such as the Aurobindo ashram in Pondicherry. Whatever its size, an ashram fulfils many functions, being a place for teaching, for the practice of yoga and meditation, and for study and prayer.

It is perhaps finally worth considering whether it is possible to be a genuine mystic without the support and intervention of a teacher.

One might argue that there is no significant difference between learning about mysticism and learning about anything else in life. Some people are naturally talented at an activity and require little tuition, whereas others benefit enormously from a coach or trainer. Others may argue however, that the mystical quest is somewhat different from ordinary practical and academic activities.

The outcome is so tenuous and subtle, on the one hand, that it may be regarded as vital to have someone to initiate the person into the relevant practices and interpretation of experience. On the other hand, there are examples of individuals with very strong mystical tendencies who appear to be largely self-taught. Mahatma Gandhi, to be considered next, perhaps falls into this category.

THE MYSTIC WITHIN THE SECULAR WORLD: THE CASE OF GANDHI

As we have explored the traditional view of the mystic within different religious traditions, we now turn to an interesting question, that of whether one can be a mystic while living a 'normal' secular life. To a large extent this flies in the face of the ideal type of mystic described in the introduction. It poses the question of whether there is any fundamental contradiction in terms between living an ordinary life, working at a job or career and perhaps having a family, and at the same time, being a seeker after mystical experience. Let us explore this question, by examining the life and spiritual beliefs of Mohandas Karamchand Gandhi or 'Mahatma' Gandhi as he is commonly known.

Gandhi was brought up as an orthodox Hindu, and in 1888 at the age of 18 decided to take up the opportunity to study law in London. He began to take an interest in religious ideas, quite apart from those of his own religion. Upon graduating as a lawyer, he returned to India yet had great difficulty in finding employment. Gandhi decided to move to South Africa where he had the promise of work. It was here that he gradually began to systematize his philosophy of life, combining his religious ideas and in particular his devotion to the Hindu scripture, the Bhagavad Gita, and his views of social justice. He found himself in South Africa working under a political regime which treated migrants from the Indian subcontinent as second-class citizens, and where there were few realistic opportunities to challenge the political system and its discriminatory laws. Gandhi mounted campaigns of civil disobedience, inspired by his reading of the Bhagavad Gita, and also of his philosophy of ahimsa, or non-violence. The latter concept is firmly rooted in the philosophies of Hinduism and Jainism, and Gandhi used it as the underlying principle of his campaigns for social justice. The principle of non-violence was on the one hand, a moral and spiritual principle to which Gandhi was devoted, but on the other hand, it became a very effective basis for a political campaign for social equality. The demonstrations by groups of Indian workers against the unfair laws in South Africa were always peaceful and conducted in accord with the principle of ahimsa. Despite the violence used against them by the South African authorities, the demonstrators never retaliated. This was perhaps the first main example of Gandhi combining a spiritual principle with direct political action.

Gandhi then returned to India, and became involved in similar kinds of social action. A celebrated example was at Champaran in the state of Bihar, where the local indigo farmers were living in extremely difficult conditions, and were exploited by a very unfair economic system. Gandhi embarked on a programme of direct, non-violent protest, and managed to a limited extent, to improve the conditions under which the indigo farmers worked. Gandhi was by now very well known, and was drawn more and more into the campaign for independence in India. However, throughout these very difficult and challenging times, he continued to be motivated by his religious and spiritual beliefs.

Although very much committed to Hinduism and in particular to the Bhagavad Gita, Gandhi was always willing to admit the failings of his religion. In particular he was greatly opposed to the social injustices brought about by the caste system, and to the great difficulties faced by the untouchables. Although he remained committed to Hinduism, he read widely about other religions, and felt that in a spiritual sense he was also aligned with all the other main world religions. His philosophical position was that there was an element of truth in all of the main world faiths.

One of the greatest truths for Gandhi was that of non-violence. This is a philosophy which is present in one form or another in all of the world's religions, but has perhaps been raised to a more sophisticated level in the religions which have evolved in India. Non-violence is regarded in such religions not simply as an absence of aggression, and an absence of doing violence to another human being. It is first of all extended to all life forms including the humblest of micro-organisms. This is evident for example, in the tradition of the Jains in not becoming involved in occupations which might harm any living creature. However, non-violence is also considered to be an absence of say verbal aggression to people, and also importantly, of not supporting a social system which permitted some sectors of society to live in poverty and degrading conditions.

It is here that Gandhi made the connection between a religious philosophy and a moral philosophy of how human beings ought to interact, with a way of undertaking direct political action. In the long struggle for Indian independence in the 1930s and 1940s, Gandhi continually advocated a policy of non-violence. His followers were subject to violent attacks resulting in death and injury, and he himself was imprisoned on a number of occasions. Despite this, he always recommended a non-violent resistance to the authorities, and argued that in effect, it was a much more powerful political weapon than violent retaliation. The 1930 demonstration in which Gandhi and his followers walked to the sea to collect salt was another example of non-violent protest. The government had imposed a high tax on salt and rather than try to pay the inflated prices, Gandhi recommended that his followers undertake a symbolic peace march to the coast, to collect their own salt. In the final analysis, Gandhi's calm, non-violent policies won the respect of the British government. Throughout the many years of protest and imprisonment, Gandhi was supported by his religious belief, reading and rereading the Bhagavad Gita as a source of inspiration, praying and meditating. One can thus argue that Gandhi, amid the turmoil of his political campaigns, sustained a religious belief and mystical practice which resulted in his being regarded as a saint in India. Gandhi's philosophy of non-violence was also extended to that of satyagraha, approximately translated as the force of truth. This term represented the idea that non-violence should not be used merely in support of any political end, but only to support those actions which were designed to eliminate unfairness and injustice in society.

Just as mystics have always tried to do, Gandhi attempted to simplify his life in as many ways as possible. He exhibited strong tendencies towards asceticism, particularly in terms of the food he ate and the clothing he wore. He had always lived within the tradition of vegetarianism, and throughout his life attempted to reduce his intake of food to his most basic requirements. In terms of clothing, he had, in South Africa, worn very conventional Western clothing, but on his return to India decided to adopt the dhoti and other forms of dress of the ordinary Indian. Moreover, during the campaign against the British, Gandhi realized the extent to which Britain controlled the cotton industry, and hence urged Indians to spin their own cloth, with which to make clothes. Gandhi was often seen at his ashram working at his own small spinning wheel.

Despite his love for tranquillity, meditation and spiritual reflection, Gandhi was, through his moral leadership of the independence movement in India, at the very heart of one of the greatest political events of the twentieth century. When independence finally came in August 1947 Gandhi was personally devastated by the internecine troubles and riots which accompanied the partition of India. In particular, the resulting mass migration of people, and the many thousands of deaths, weighed upon him as a very heavy burden. Throughout all this period however, he continued to pray, to meditate and to read the Bhagavad Gita. He was thus a remarkable example of a mystic, who lived his life not in seclusion, but in the very heart of social and political turmoil he used his religious and mystical insights, to help him to act according to his own principles in the most testing of times. One might argue that although the life of a mystic is no doubt arduous and challenging in both a physical and spiritual sense, it is arguably even more so if one has test one's spiritual principles in an atmosphere of great stress and tension. It is perhaps one thing to approach God in a quiet place, far away from the rush of life, but another to do so during a period of intense danger and communal violence.

In analysing the lifestyles of mystics therefore, we can often see a trend towards withdrawal from the world, but in many cases, there is also an apparent urge to act upon the world, and to improve as much as possible, some of the ills of society. We will review later, another example of this need for moral intervention in the world, in the life of Simone Weil.

KEY IDEAS

When we examine the lifestyle of mystics in different religious traditions, we can identify a number of common trends in the way they live, for example, a tendency to withdraw from the world, to abstain from material pleasures, and to undergo periodic fasting. Some of these practices have become established in orthodox religious tradition, for example, in the final stage of withdrawal from the world in the classical Hindu model of the stages of life. Fasting during the month of Ramadan is an essential aspect of Islamic religious observance. In some religions there is the example of a lineage of mystical or spiritual teachers, for example, in Sikhism and in Zen Buddhism. Some mystics however appear to be able to combine the spiritual life with a practical life in the secular world.

PART II

THE TRADITIONS OF MYSTICISM

CHAPTER 4

BUDDHIST MYSTICISM

SUMMARY

This chapter examines those aspects of the Buddhist religion which could be regarded as mystical. It could be argued, for example, that the entire religion is fundamentally mystical in nature, and this proposition will be analysed. The chapter will begin with a broad overview of mysticism throughout the Buddhist tradition. There will then be an examination of the mystical elements within two Buddhist Schools, those of the Zen tradition within Japan, and the Tibetan Vajrayana tradition. The chapter will conclude with a review of the contributions of D. T. Suzuki and of Chagdud Tulku Rinpoche.

INTRODUCTION

Buddhism is not a mystical religion in the sense that it involves or aspires to a sense of merger or unity with a single, all-powerful, creator God. There is no such concept in Buddhism, and hence the idea of mystical activity lies in a different direction. One of the purposes of Buddhism could be described as the identification of the true nature of the self, or of the individual. This process involves the understanding of the relationship which we have with the world around us, and how we interrelate with the rest of the organic and inorganic world. This understanding, however, is intended to exist in a balanced and objective way, so that if we were to achieve this goal as a Buddhist, we would fully understand who we were, unaffected by subjective feelings of what we might prefer to be, or what we would ideally like the world to be. In a sense then, the union which is characteristic of Buddhism is not union with some external entity, but a union with the fully conscious reality of who we actually are.

To put it briefly, and hopefully not too simplistically, the goal of Buddhism is to become an accurate reflection of our true nature. A corollary to this is that in learning to appreciate the nature of our own humanity, we also understand that of others. Buddhists would argue that this helps us to more fully comprehend the nature of all human existence and hence to develop a closer sense of empathy with others.

THE BUDDHA'S TEACHINGS

For the historical Buddha, the north Indian prince, Siddhartha Gautama, the starting point for this search for one's true self, was the existence of suffering, whether this was physical in nature resulting from say illness, or whether it arose from psychological sources. Fundamentally, the Buddha's response to the existence of suffering, and to its consequences for us, was that although we may not be able to eliminate the cause of the suffering, we can do something about our mental response to it. In other words, if we are suffering from a dangerous illness, we may not actually be able to achieve a cure for the illness, but if we can adjust our mental attitude and response to the illness, then we may reduce or even eliminate the suffering which results from the illness. So for example, some of the pain from illness results from our feelings of frustration and irritation that we cannot do the things we want to do. We compare ourselves with healthy people, and feel a sense of unfairness that we have been afflicted.

The Buddha summed up the phenomenon of suffering in a suc-cinct manner in what are known as the Four Noble Truths. The first Truth is that the existence of suffering is an empirical reality. We simply cannot imagine any individual human being, or community, where there is an absence of suffering. Even if we are extremely for-tunate, and have a broadly trouble-free and pleasant life, we all have to die. Very few of us wish to leave this world, particularly if we have enjoyed our lives. The process of dying involves suffering, partly because it may be physically painful, partly because there is a sense of permanence about it, and also because we can often see the suffer-ing our dying creates in others. Hence, the first Truth is to accept the almost universal existence of suffering of various kinds.

The second Truth is that there is a source to this suffering, or at least a factor which makes this suffering worse than it need be. This factor is not the physical illness, or the actual fact of dying, but our response to it. The fundamental response of the vast majority of people to the experience of suffering is that we want the suffering to go away. If we are ill, we badly want to get better. If we are told we have a serious, or indeed terminal, illness, we want some intervention to prevent our dying. If we are very anxious about something, then we want the cause of that anxiety to disappear. In other words we are continually wanting the world to change for the better, to cause us less distress. We are seldom happy with the way the world is. If we have just got a new car, it does not take us very long, before we are admiring the even bigger, new car owned by our neighbour. We are always, as human beings, wanting things. As parents we want our children to be successful; as employees we are always wanting a promotion, and as house-owners we are always wanting a better house with a bigger garden. For the Buddha, this continual feeling of desire, of wanting things to be better, was at the root cause of suffering.

The third Noble Truth is that it is possible, in principle to reduce this sense of desire, and hence to minimize suffering. The final Noble Truth is the way that the Buddha proposed to achieve this. In other words, the final Truth, is that the reduction or elimination of desire, is not impossible, but can actually be achieved through a process developed by the Buddha. This method consists of eight separate, yet interlinked procedures, termed the Noble Eightfold Path.

The first three stages of this strategy may not seem particularly different to approaches in other religions. They broadly refer to ways of conducting one's life in an ethical manner. The first step is described as Right Speech, indicating that we should always try to avoid causing offence to others by things that we say. In addition, we should always try to be honest and truthful in the way we describe things, and should adopt a manner of speaking which is calm and pleasant to others. The second moral stage of Right Actions indicates that we should always try to behave in such a way that we do not harm other beings, and are kind and supportive to them. It is basically concerned with behaving in a positive, constructive and supportive manner. Right Livelihood is concerned with having an occupation which does not involve harm to others, and does not exploit other people in any way. Of course, in practice, it may not be possible to achieve these aims perfectly, but the Buddhist philosophy is to aspire to these moral conditions, and to at least through speech, action and livelihood, try to live in harmony with our fellow human beings, and the planet at large.

The remainder of the Noble Eightfold Path is perhaps more distinctively Buddhist, and involves strategies which are ultimately designed to avoid suffering, and to help the individual appreciate more clearly, the reality of existence. The next element in the Path can be described as Right Effort. This signifies that spiritual progress is not something which comes easily. The aspirant must be conscious that his or her life and understanding of the world can be changed for the better, and that the only way to achieve this is to work very hard at the necessary strategies. The Buddha's approach requires regular discipline and effort to succeed. Right Mindfulness refers to the need to be focused on the events around us at all times, so that we do not act in a casual or thoughtless fashion. It is very easy for human beings to do things in a semi-automatic manner without actually thinking about what we are doing. When we behave in this way, the things that we do have very little significance because we do not consider them sufficiently carefully before we act. Linked to this is the idea of Right Concentration, whereby we train our minds to focus upon the present moment, and do not let our minds wander off to unnecessary or harmful thoughts. This is a central element in Buddhist training, and one that is key in developing a frame of reference within which we can adopt a wiser view of the world. Through the use of these techniques we can develop a sense of Right Understanding, or a more objective and balanced perspective upon the world. Normally human beings have a tendency to attach importance to things which are really not very important, and vice versa. They have a distorted view of the world, and a major element of Buddhist training is to remedy that. Once a clearer understanding of the nature of existence was developed, the individual is able to have Right Thoughts, or to look at the world with a totally balanced objectivity, unaffected by the desire to change it or to make it more suited to their own perceived needs and wishes. In a sense, it can be argued that all the eight aspects of this path are mutually dependent and interlinked. One cannot really focus upon one or two elements and forget the others. It is also important to remember that the Eightfold Path is a discipline, in that however experienced and practiced a person may be in the principles of Buddhism, one has to continue striving and practising all one's life. Buddhism is not a doctrine in which one is asked to believe and have faith. Rather it is a method which one is invited to try, and to experience the results.

One of the key aspects of reality which can be learned through the Buddhist discipline is that of impermanence. We often tend to think about the world as if it will continue for ever, without recognizing sufficiently that it is continually changing. Within the environmental movement there is now an acknowledgement that we cannot accept that the world is permanent. We recognize that if we do not care for the planet that it could be permanently damaged. The Buddhist analysis however, can be applied not only at the level of the planet, but on a much smaller personal level. Everything around us, whether living or non-living, will one day cease to exist. Living things die and are replaced by other living things. Rocks, or even mountains, are slowly eroded, and finally end as dust particles. Grand buildings either disintegrate gradually, or are destroyed by human intervention. According to Buddhists, once we truly understand the all-embracing nature of impermanence, then this changes our attitude towards the world. We do not become so attached to material possessions because by doing so we become overly concerned with things which are ultimately unimportant. If we are wealthy and have a great many valuable possessions, it is easy to become obsessed with guarding them, and protecting them, as if they are totally permanent. Buddhists argue that such a frame of mind can be very stressful, and generate a distorted view of reality.

A different although related perspective on non-attachment is connected with the way in which we perceive ourselves. If we are very successful, either in terms of say our jobs or in an activity such as sport, we often tend to feel very proud, and to think how well 'we' have done. In other words, we focus very much on ourselves as an individual, thinking that our success is a reflection of the individual within us. It tends to be a very ego-centred perception of success. Now Buddhists would argue that there is nothing really to which we can attach this success. Buddhists would ask us to consider where the 'I' within us is located. Is it in the brain, or perhaps the heart, or somewhere else? This is of course a very difficult question to answer. The Buddhist response is that there is not actually an 'I' or a self, in any meaningful way, and that our obsession with the 'self' leads to a distorted sense of attachment, and concern for things which are really impermanent. The ideas of impermanence, non-attachment and of no-self are central to the Buddhist analysis of existence. A further consequence of the idea of no-self is that as we think less about the notion of an 'I', we tend not to look out at the world from the point of view of 'I' as an individual, looking at the rest of humanity. If there are no 'I' s or 'me's among human beings, then there is much more a sense of shared humanity. We do not think I am 'right' and others are 'wrong' because there is no 'I' to be right.

There is no sense in this discussion then, that Buddhism involves any kind of union or merger with an all-powerful force in the universe. Quite the opposite in fact. The Buddha's analysis of the human condition is that salvation for human beings, if salvation is an appropriate word, lies in the hands of the individual person. The Buddha does not suggest looking externally for help, but rather trying to discipline and control our own minds, and hence develop a healthier and more balanced perspective on the world. This more balanced perspective will help us to live happier and more fulfilled lives. In so doing, we are helped to make contact with what we might term our true, original, essential nature. We become one with the best and most natural elements within us. Normally, we lose touch with this original element of ourselves because we become attached to the more trivial and peripheral elements of life. However, by following the Buddhist discipline, we regain contact with our true nature as human beings, or perhaps we might say our essential humanity. Therein lies the mystical in Buddhism. The relocation of our true nature is the ultimate mystical quest in Buddhism. To achieve it is to be enlightened.

Like all great religions, Buddhism has changed and adapted within different cultural contexts, while at the same time retaining the essential elements of its teaching. We shall now examine two traditions, which externally may appear rather different. These are the Zen tradition of Japan and the Tibetan Buddhist tradition. However, despite apparent differences, they share the fundamental Buddhist principles, and the pursuit of what is essentially a mystical quest.

THE ZEN TRADITION

The origins of Zen Buddhism, and indeed its essential character, are reputed to be capable of being traced back to a particular event in the life of the historical Buddha. The Buddha frequently gathered his followers together to teach them and discuss some aspect of his principles of practice. On one particular day he is said to have held up a flower to show to the gathered disciples. The Buddha offered no explanation of his action, but merely held the flower for all to see. As might be expected his disciples were generally puzzled by this, but one disciple named Mahakasyapa understood what the Buddha was indicating with the flower. In someway the disciple made clear to the Buddha that he understood, and the Buddha then made clear to the audience that he had given a specific teaching to the monk. This teaching could not be found in any scriptures, and was to be passed on from the monk to others, directly, and in an experiential way. In other words, people could only understand this specific Buddhist teaching by living closely with a teacher, and by absorbing the teaching through careful observation of the teacher's lifestyle. This style of Zen tuition has continued to this day.

This particular tradition was passed on from Mahakasyapa to a number of other Buddhist teachers in succession. Eventually the teaching was transmitted to a monk named Bodhidharma who, in approximately the early sixth century CE, carried the teachings of Zen from India to China. In China this particular tradition became known as Chan Buddhism, whereas when it was eventually carried to Japan, it became known as Zen.

When we spoke above about the mystical nature of Buddhism, in terms of finding our original nature, and looking within for the very best and most noble qualities which we possess, this is in someways specifically what Zen aims to do. In the Zen tradition, this inner nature is known as the Buddha nature. Zen practitioners believe that all human beings possess this Buddha nature, but that it is easier with some people than with others, to release these qualities, and to identify with this inner nature. Moreover, Zen practitioners believe that the finding of the Buddha nature can be achieved by means of meditation, and of a kind of non-rational exploration of the world. There tends to be little emphasis upon the written scriptures, simply because it is believed these tend to encourage a form of rational, logical reasoning which is antithetical to the Zen approach. In fact, members of the Zen tradition try to emulate the strategies and techniques employed by the Buddha in reaching enlightenment. They argue that the Buddha did not read scriptures and think logically about their contents to try to reach enlightenment. Quite the contrary, he employed very practical techniques of meditation and mindfulness. Particularly in monastic communities, this is also accompanied by long periods of manual labour around the monastery, intended to be conducted in a very focused and mindful way.

The primary method of meditation in Zen is called zazen (Suzuki, 2004). This is a form of group meditation, in which the practitioner normally adopts the sitting lotus position. Sometimes monks and nuns sit facing a blank wall, and on other occasions they may face the centre of a room, perhaps sitting in a straight line. They will typically commence a meditation session by 'watching' the breath. This is a general technique often used in Buddhism, where one counts the breaths, or perhaps concentrates on the breath coming and going from the tip of the nostrils. Some approaches to Zen training then advocate the quiet watching of thoughts as they arise and fall within consciousness. Other Zen traditions employ a verbal conundrum given to the aspirant by a teacher. The student has to reflect upon the conundrum, which is expressed in such a way as to eliminate the possibility of rational thought. This conundrum or koan in a sense forces the individual to reject a logical solution to the problem. This technique is said to assist the individual in locating the elusive Buddha nature (Isshu and Sasaki, 1993).

An example of a koan is the question 'Does a dog possess a Buddha-nature?' The Zen teacher or master will in the first place give the Zen student a koan upon which to reflect. From time to time, often in a formal context, the teacher may ask the student for the latest thoughts on the koan. This is designed to make an estimate of the student's progress. There is in fact, no single correct response to a particular koan. A response may be judged correct in one context at one time, but in a different situation, another student may find that the same response is rejected. The Zen teacher is considering both the response, but also the way in which it is given. In particular, the teacher is looking for evidence that the student has begun to understand the reality of the world more clearly, particularly in terms of the impermanence and unsatisfactoriness of existence.

Zen places great emphasis upon the idea of impermanence, mentioned earlier. On a philosophical level, Zen perceives the world as being composed of innumerable different elements. These elements are recombined into the physical world that we see around us. The physical world includes human beings, trees, buildings, and indeed everything that makes up what we think of as the everyday world. However, this combination of elements into an object or a living thing does not last for ever. Ultimately it is destined to disaggregate, whereupon the object will gradually fall apart and cease to exist, and the living thing will die. Nevertheless, new objects will be created and new living things will be born. Once we recognize that this is the nature of all phenomena in the world, then it becomes very difficult to be deeply attached to either objects or living things. The world of phenomena is but a temporary construction.

Moreover, according to this philosophy the 'natural' state of the world is really one in which things are disaggregated. This explains the significance of the concept of 'emptiness' in Zen philosophy. Once we truly appreciate this philosophy, we recognize that we can empty the mind of attachments to 'things', and hence bring ourselves closer to this naturally 'empty' condition of the world. This is one of the reasons for the pre-eminence of space and emptiness in Zen art, painting and calligraphy. In paintings, tiny figures in a landscape are juxtaposed with the emptiness of vast skies. In a Zen garden, large areas of empty, raked sand represent this emptiness; and in calligraphy, the writing is often located alone on a large sheet of paper with much empty space.

One consequence of the realization that phenomena consist of temporary aggregations of matter is that we may become much less inclined to be discriminatory or to choose one thing rather than another. Once we recognize that all the things before us, whether animate or inanimate, are but temporary phenomena, it seems less necessary to treat one as desirable and the other as undesirable. After all, if the world and universe is fundamentally a single integrated whole, from which phenomena are but temporary creations, then being too selective or choosy seems a little unnecessary. Followers of Zen may thus become much more accepting of the world. They perhaps do not respond too quickly when things appear not to be going well, or indeed when they are going well. They regard the world with a certain kind of calm, equanimity.

One way of defining enlightenment then is when someone fully appreciates the true nature of the living and non-living world, in relation to the universe as a whole. When someone fully realizes that all aggregated entities are destined to decay and disintegrate, and that person is thus not attached to them, then one might say that such a person is enlightened. The ultimate purpose of Zen training is to help the individual bring about that realization.

Finally, to restate the mystical nature of Zen in a slightly different way, one could say that the realization that we as human beings are simply temporary aggregates of matter, and that we bear the same relationship to the whole as do other members of the natural and physical world, then that awareness is synonymous with the mystical experience in Zen.

We now examine a somewhat esoteric tradition in Buddhism known as the Vajrayana.

VAJRAYANA

Vajrayana belongs to the overall Mahayana Buddhist tradition, of which Zen is also a part. Vajrayana is particularly associated with the Himalaya region, including the countries of Tibet, Nepal and Bhutan. The main purpose of the Vajrayana is to enable the mystic to achieve enlightenment much more quickly than by conventional means. This is done in two principal ways. First a range of esoteric techniques are employed, which are not readily available outside the limits of certain Tantric Buddhist groups; secondly, Vajrayana, indeed like Zen, uses the guidance of an experienced teacher to help the aspirant make progress. It is claimed that by these methods, an individual aspirant may be able to gain enlightenment very rapidly.

The role of the guru is very important in Vajrayana, and a close relationship very often develops between disciple and guru. A tantric method which is often associated with Tibet, and described in the Bardo Thodol or Tibetan Book of the Dead, entails using the process of dying, as a vehicle whereby the individual may attain enlightenment (Coleman and Jinpa, 2005). Meditation and other techniques are employed to achieve this aim, and it is claimed that the mind is particularly sensitive to such practises at the time of death. This tradition describes a number of different conscious or semi-conscious states between the period of dying and the period of being reborn. The Bardo Thodol describes methods which can be used to make spiritual progress during these states. Some other tantric practices actually entail the worship and performance of ceremonies before the statue of a deity. This is unusual within orthodox Buddhist tradition, since the Buddha made it perfectly clear that he did not wish to assume the role of any kind of deity.

The ultimate aim of the Vajrayana is to attain enlightenment and particularly to use this understanding of the reality of the world to assist other mystics in achieving this state. The state of being enlightened is sometimes known as Buddhahood. There is also within Tibetan Buddhism the important concept of the Bodhisattva. This is a person who either has already attained enlightenment, or who perhaps has progressed a considerable way towards that goal, and who uses his or her knowledge to assist others towards the goal of escaping the endless cycle of rebirths. Within the tradition, people are encouraged to commit themselves to the goal of assisting others in achieving enlightenment. There is within Tibetan Buddhism in general, and also to some extent within Vajrayana, a tendency to engage in personal reflection on the teachings of Buddhism, and indeed to check the teachings against not only logical thought but also empirical experience. In other words, practitioners will ask themselves whether the teachings they have received are actually compatible with their experiences of meditation or of life in general. This is not a negative tendency, but merely a reflection of the rationality of the Buddhist teachings. Nevertheless, it should not be thought that this tradition reflects negative attitudes towards Buddhist teachers. The guru or lama is very highly regarded, and aspirants hold their teacher in very high esteem.

Learning about Vajrayana techniques, however, is not necessarily as straightforward as in some other Buddhist traditions. Teachings are not necessarily passed on in their totality to aspirants. The student is judged in terms of their capability of receiving a particular teaching, and teachings are not transmitted until the aspirant is considered ready to receive them. The Vajrayana tradition also includes an important process of initiation, and potential students are warned not to attempt to commence study of Vajrayana until they have received appropriate initiation.

Tantra forms an essential element of Vajrayana practice (Yeshe, 1987). Tantric methods are found in both Hinduism and Buddhism, and in both religions tend to constitute an esoteric tradition within the main religion. As a phenomenon, tantra is so diverse that it is difficult to define, but central to the approach is the adaptation and utilization of the spiritual energy of the universe, for the spiritual benefit of the individual. According to the philosophy of tantra, all human beings possess a degree of this universal energy within them, but generally do not know how to utilize it. The tantric approach enables the individual, through a variety of rites and practices, to take advantage of the universal spiritual energy within themselves. Although the Vajrayana as a tradition is normally associated with Tibetan Buddhism, the Shingon School of Buddhism based in Japan is also related to Vajrayana. In Shingon Buddhism, there is the same emphasis upon the possibility of a rapid approach to enlightenment using many of the same practices as in Tibetan Vajrayana, that is, mystical diagrams such as yantra, spiritual symbols such as mantra, and the use of meditational techniques.

We will now examine two case studies of exponents of Buddhism, namely, D. T. Suzuki to represent the Zen School, and Chagdud Tulku Rinpoche, to represent Vajrayana Buddhism.

DAISETZ TEITARO SUZUKI

Dr Suzuki was probably the first, and certainly the best-known writer and teacher to spread widely the Zen philosophy and practice in the West. During a period when most people outside Japan had little knowledge or awareness of Zen, Suzuki brought, through his books and lectures, an understanding of Zen meditation and teachings, which led to the widespread interest in the tradition in Europe and the United States.

Suzuki was born in 1870 and died in 1966. In his youth he was a student of the celebrated Zen teacher, Shaku Soen, and also for a time, studied Theravada Buddhism in Sri Lanka. In the late nineteenth century he visited the United States, and as an excellent linguist he was asked to help with the translation of many Buddhist works into English. He subsequently held professorial appointments and became a leading figure in the academic study of Zen. He developed an interest in Western Christian mystical traditions, and made comparative studies of mysticism in the West and in Japan. He was also very interested in the historical interaction between Zen and Japanese culture, and the manner in which they had mutually influenced each other.

CHAGDUD TULKU RINPOCHE

Chagdud Tulku was born in 1930 in eastern Tibet, and died in 2003. He was a well-known teacher of the Vajrayana tradition, and was also influential in bringing an understanding of Tibetan Buddhism to the West. As a young boy he received an intensive education and training in the Buddhist tradition involving long periods of supervised meditation. He was 29 years of age when China invaded Tibet in 1959, and he succeeded in escaping to India, where he lived in a number of different Tibetan refugee camps. He became more and more in demand as a teacher of the Vajrayana tradition, and after some time he obtained permission to enter the United States. While there he established meditation centres and also a book publishing organization. Throughout his life he maintained an energetic programme of establishing or encouraging others to establish centres for the study of the Tibetan tradition. He remained deeply committed to the principle of assisting other people to strive towards the enlightened condition.

KEY IDEAS

Although there is great diversity in Buddhist practice within different cultures, and great diversity in external patterns of religion, there remains a remarkable consistency in the nature of the teaching, and in the mystical nature of the aims of the spiritual practice. The Buddha outlined the essential problems of existence, and then proceeded to indicate a way to resolve these problems. His method culminated in helping people to understand the true nature of reality, and to appreciate the relationship of the individual with the totality of the universe. This fundamentally mystical understanding is at the heart of Buddhism and is termed enlightenment. The individual is brought to an understanding of the impermanent nature of the world, and of the consequences for human beings. Once we truly understand the nature of impermanence, then we are able to reduce or eliminate the extent of our attachment to the world.

CHAPTER 5

SUFISM

SUMMARY

This chapter examines the main teachings and approaches of Sufism, and explores the relationship between the Sufi teacher or shaykh, and the aspirant. It discusses the methods used by Sufis to attain a deeper knowledge of God, and the relationship between Sufi practice and orthodox, traditional Islam. The idea of asceticism and relinquishing the material things of the world has always been significant in Sufism, and this is explored in the lives of several Sufis. The nature of the ultimate goal of Sufi mysticism is discussed, and the Sufi experience is then explored within the context of two case studies of the lives of Jalal-e-Din Rumi, and of Rabia al-Basri, a celebrated woman Sufi mystic.

INTRODUCTION

Sufism is the mystical tradition within Islam, and represents a major strand of thought and practice within the religion. The consensus within Islam would appear to be that one is initially a Muslim, and thereafter, if one wishes, one attaches oneself to the Sufi tradition. The most widely accepted account of the origin of the word Sufism is that it is derived from the Arabic word, suf, meaning wool. The early Sufi mystics probably wore coarsely spun cloaks made of wool, and this is the assumed explanation for the origin of the word. Sufism as a practice and belief system, very much, relies upon the personal tuition of a shaykh or spiritual leader. The teachings of Sufism pass back in a line of succession to the prophet Muhammad, and there is very much a sense in which the transmission of teachings should be achieved on a personal level, through one-to-one communication

(Knysh, 2000). Although the standard teachings of Islam remain very important and relevant within the Sufi tradition, there is this historical emphasis upon one-to-one teaching, from master to student.

THE ROLE OF THE SHAYKH

The aim of Sufism is to achieve a very close, personal relationship with God. This goal is achieved through a long and intense period of personal training through the tuition of a shaykh. The relationship between the Sufi aspirant and the shaykh is a very close one. It does not involve simply the transmission of knowledge and skills, or the techniques necessary for making spiritual progress. The relationship is also of a close, personal nature. The student will very rarely change his or her shaykh, and the connection will normally remain for the rest of their respective lives. The shaykh has a very close personal investment in the spiritual development of the student.

Clearly there will come a time when the aspirant has developed to a stage where he can leave the shaykh, and when the shaykh authorizes him to teach others as a Sufi master himself. However, even though the aspirant, now a shaykh, may have his own students, the relationship with his original teacher will always remain, and he may continue to take advice from him. There is clearly a sense of continuity here leading backwards in history through a series of spiritual teachers to the prophet Muhammad. Clearly also, the tradition progresses, so that masters teach students, who in their turn become shaykhs and then teach others themselves. The individual nature of the tuition will differ from teacher to teacher, but it may well involve long periods of routine physical or community work. Part of the purpose of these long periods of duty is to help eliminate in the aspirant, a sense of the subjective individual.

It is considered within Sufism that one of the principal characteristics which stands in the way of spiritual development is a sense of the ego. Service to others, and routine physical work, help at least partially to overcome feelings of egotism and self-importance. The shaykh will often be the spiritual leader of a tariqah or specific order of Sufis. As such he will guide the spiritual development of the members of the order, and act generally as a spiritual leader. A well-known Sufi order is the Naqshbandi order, which derives its tradition via Abu Bakr to the prophet Muhammad (Trimingham, 1971).

It is probably important to note however, that Sufism should not be viewed as a collection of spiritual techniques, which if followed assiduously will lead to a form of enlightened state or mystical consciousness. It is considered important within Sufism that the aspirant is a devoted Muslim, and complies with all the requirements of the religion. In a sense, this is the basis of being a Sufi. The Quran remains the essential source of spiritual truth for a Sufi, as for Muslims more generally. Nevertheless, some Sufis would seek for perhaps more complex spiritual meanings in the Quran in keeping with their mystical quest, rather than perhaps the more straightforward interpretation. The practices advocated by the shaykh come after this providing a spiritual tradition and practice which builds upon a firm basis in orthodox Islam. The potential for shaykhs to offer teachings which are to some extent different from the norm, and may even, in the eyes of some, contradict established Islamic teachings, has sometimes created the possibility of conflict within Islam.

RELIGIOUS PRACTICE

Of the many practices adopted by Sufis, one of the best known is that of dhikr or the concentration of the mind on God. This may be achieved in a variety of ways, but is normally done by the repetition of the name or names of God. Dhikr may be performed silently, or it may be spoken or performed to the accompaniment of music or dance. However, there have been conflicting opinions about the acceptability of dhikr combined with music. Some feel that dhikr should be performed simply by remembering the name of God through verbal repetition. This is a form of meditation and mind concentration, but the purpose throughout is to focus the mind of the person upon God. Many Sufis use sets of beads to help them repeat the name of God. There are often 99 beads on a single string. However, some Muslims prefer to use the system of counting upon the fingers of the hand. Under the guidance of a spiritual teacher, the practice of dhikr sometimes involves forms of breath control and breathing meditation .In some Sufi orders, dhikr is an element of a more complex ceremony involving singing and music.

The ultimate purpose of the practice of dhikr is the attainment of fana, or a sense of escape from the obsessions with the material world. For the Sufi, the process of spiritual purification requires a gradual elimination of concerns for the world which surrounds us, and an absolute concentration upon God and the spiritual life. It is a process of eliminating all concern with the self. The concept of the 'I' is seen as encouraging a preoccupation with that which seems attractive and pleasurable in the material world, rather than in focusing upon the Sufi spiritual discipline and the virtues of the religious life.

As part of this process, there has tended throughout the history of Sufism to be a concern with poverty and a rejection of the material world, as an important feature of spiritual progress. Poverty on its own, however, was not regarded as an automatic feature of spiritual progress. It was in a sense, a means to an end. It was one element on the road to a life of spiritual purity, which would in due course lead to a closeness with God. Generally, some Sufis may argue that an absence of worldly goods helps the aspirant to eliminate feelings of pride and acquisitiveness, which would be obstacles on the mystical path to God.

Within Islam, the shariah traditionally provides the framework for the orthodox system of Islamic belief and practice, while the tariqa or Sufi 'way' provides an inner, perhaps more intrinsic understanding of spiritual truth. The word tariqa can also be employed to indicate a specific way as embodied in a particular Sufi order. It is important to stress however, that the Sufi should obey the requirements of the shariah, since this represents the fundamentals of Islamic belief. Only then can the aspirant progress to the arguably more complex and sophisticated understandings of the tariqa. Many would therefore argue that Sufis have a responsibility to give primacy to the basic teachings of Islam, and to support the community of believers. Only when this is supported and achieved, should mystics progress on their spiritual journey.

This particular philosophy of Sufism is very much reflected in the approach of the Persian mystic, Al-Ghazali. He was born in the city of Tus in 1058 CE and died there in 1111 CE. He was very well educated as a young man, and later became an eminent university professor who was held in great esteem. His writing and teaching made him very famous. However, in middle age he had a crisis of confidence in the path which he had chosen. He certainly became physically ill, although one might hypothesize whether the illness initiated his evaluation of his life, or whether his spiritual and intellectual crisis brought on a period of ill-health. It appears that he had personally and privately begun to question whether his successful academic career was what he really wanted. He began to feel that if he was really honest with himself, then the prime motivation for pursuing his academic career was the pride he felt in his success and position. In other words he was very attached to the status which success had brought him. He appears not to have eliminated his attachment to the material world, and to the 'I', which reflected a preoccupation with the physical rather than spiritual world.

He decided that if he was to achieve true spiritual enlightenment and know God directly, then he had to break with his present life-style. He therefore decided to adopt a Sufi lifestyle and to lead a wandering life. He went first on a pilgrimage to Mecca, but then spent over ten years in travelling in Syria and in Palestine, writing, meditating and living the life of a wandering mendicant. Eventually, however, he returned to Tus and founded a small centre for the study of Sufi principles. Al-Ghazali was always a devout Muslim in the conventional sense, and yet, beyond that, he felt that rational and intellectual study could only take one so far in the pursuit of a mysti-cal apprehension of God. He considered that ultimately one had to learn experientially about God, rather than from the study of books.

There are some interesting philosophical questions here about the nature of the Sufi endeavour. First, some might argue that as the Quran and the shariah are based upon the will of God, they repre-sent a complete means of attaining the highest spiritual development. If one takes that view, then one might suppose that Sufi mystical practices are superfluous to the core teachings of Islam. There is also the question of whether Sufism truly leads to a sense of merger with God. One might take the view that a human being with all the accom-panying imperfections should never assume to be capable of merging with the perfection of God. On the one hand, one might feel that a human being can, with spiritual training, approach very closely to God, but never actually merge with the Divine. On the other hand, one might feel that the concept of merger with God implies no more than human beings returning to their true destiny and origin.

The general question of the extent to which Sufism may claim to go beyond the religious experience of orthodox Islam is a problem-atic one. The issue was brought to a very sharp focus by the case of Al-Hallaj, the Baghdad mystic who was executed in 922 CE. In his younger days, he developed a leading reputation among some as a profound mystical thinker, and yet attained a certain notoriety among others for his apparently extreme statements about Islamic theology. He uttered, at various times, a number of enigmatic proclamations which appeared to assert his own divinity. There were conflicting opinions about whether his utterances were genuinely heretical. After much discussion lasting many years, during a considerable part of which Al-Hallaj was imprisoned, it was finally decided that he should be tried as a heretic. He was found guilty and executed. These events illustrate the problematic nature of a mystical tradition appearing to go beyond the bounds of orthodoxy. The general view is that Sufism is an element of mainstream Islam and thereby gains its legitimacy. There are hence lines beyond which it should not go. Clearly there will always be some discussion about where these lines actually lie, but broadly speaking that is the orthodox position.

The Sufi quest has traditionally involved a pathway of personal development in which one gradually aspires to simplify one's life and devote it more and more to the pursuit of God. Among other things, the Sufi tries to gradually eliminate desires for the material support of the world. The goal towards which Sufis are aiming is to regard God as a sufficient support for survival in the world. Hence, no matter how hungry, thirsty or cold one might be, the Sufi aims to learn to ignore these needs, and to have faith that when God sees fit, he will provide the necessities of life. The Sufi should thus have total confidence that God will provide what is necessary. The mystic submits his will entirely to the will of God. However, to do this it is essential that the mystic focuses upon God at all times. It is regarded as not possible to have a close relationship with God, unless one focuses upon the name of God as much as possible. Through this practice, the Sufi is said to reach a state where everything that he thinks relates to God. In other words, everything else in the physical and psychological worlds are seen only through an understanding of God. It is as if God is seen as the focus of everything, and is the subject of an intense feeling of love from the mystic. As these feelings proceed, the mystic finally abandons all sense of involvement in the self. The mystic is no longer at all concerned with his own well-being, but has experienced fana, or elimination of the concept of self. In this final stage of the Sufi experience, the mystic is totally concerned with God.

We now turn to an examination of the Sufi experience within the lives of two celebrated Sufis, Jalal-e-Din Rumi and Rabia al-Basri.

JALAL-E-DIN RUMI

Rumi lived from 1207 until 1273, and was a celebrated Sufi philosopher, poet and theologian (Schimmel, 1978). After his death, his
spiritual descendants established the Mevlevi order, which became
famous for its dervish dancing. Rumi was born in what is now
Afghanistan, but the instability of the times, including the danger of
invasions from Mongolia, caused his family to migrate westwards.
After a series of journeys, including the pilgrimage to Mecca, Rumi's
family established themselves in the city of Konya, in the Anatolia
area of what is now Turkey. Rumi's father was a very well-educated
Muslim, who was able to stimulate his son's interest in spiritual
matters. After considerable study and training, Rumi became one of
the key teachers in the mosques and madrassahs of the city. In his
mid-thirties he became accepted in the role of shaykh. The essence
and key concept of the thought of Rumi is that of union with God.
The term for this is tawhid, and is central to Sufi mystical philosophy.

Rumi cultivated friendship with a variety of spiritual teachers and
mystics in the region of Konya, and one of the most important was a
mystic named Shams. Rumi and Shams became very close, so much
so that it created friction between Rumi and his other friends. This
situation continued for some time, until eventually feelings became
so intense, that Shams was murdered. Rumi was profoundly upset by
this loss, but perhaps paradoxically it may have motivated Rumi to
some of his most intense spiritual reflections, and in particular the
writing of some of his best spiritual poetry, for which he has remained
famous.

Rumi was particularly interesting as a mystic in that he advocated
the employment of artistic practices such as poetry and dance as an
accompaniment to the spiritual life. He was particularly fascinated
by the use of music in mystical activity, and this led to his development of the idea of dance, and the 'whirling dervishes'. Within this
practice, the whirling dance was seen as a metaphor for the gradual
ascent towards a union with God. Rumi also expressed many of his
ideas in poetry, which has retained an extremely wide popularity
over the years. The fundamental essence of his approach was that he
considered that human beings had received their full potential from
God, and that they would recognize that potential by aspiring
towards a return to the Divine. It should perhaps be noted that the

use of music and dance within Sufi practice, does not probably attract the approval of all Muslims, who may regard it as moving too far from orthodox practice.

RABIA AL-BASRI

Rabia was born in approximately 717 CE, in the city of Basra, and died in 801 CE. She had three elder sisters, and the family was extremely poor. She was called Rabia by her parents as the name means 'fourth', signifying her birth as the fourth child of the family. When she was still only young her parents died, and she became a servant. It seems that she was overworked and had a very difficult life. However, she was very devout, and committed to her faith. It is said that the head of the household in which she worked became extremely impressed by the level of her devotion, and released her from what was in effect slavery. It appears that she spent some time in the desert in prayer and meditation, and at some point constructed a shelter for herself in which she spent her time in devotion to God. She is thought to have made a pilgrimage to Mecca, at about this time. Perhaps later, several key figures in the community around Basra wished to marry her, but she declined. She pointed out that she had no wish to be tied to the world of material things or to worldly commitments. She regarded herself as a true Sufi, and one who was exclusively devoted to God. Rabia was determined to remain unattached to the world, so that she could concentrate on her love for God. She had many followers and disciples, but she was very restrained in the extent to which she was prepared to assist them. One disciple apparently asked her to pray for him, yet she refused on the grounds that he did not need anyone to come between him and God. She advised him to pray directly to God.

Rabia, in common with other Sufi mystics of the period, regularly underwent privations and ascetic practices to try to come nearer to God. Rabia continually tried to accustom herself to the many physical hardships which she faced, and to conquer them. Arguably Rabia's most significant contribution to Sufi teaching was her development of the idea of love for God. She placed much less emphasis on the ideas of fearing God, and fearing retribution, and much more on having a feeling of loving devotion. Rabia appears not to have left any written records of her teaching.

KEY IDEAS

An important concept within Sufism has been the notion that the mystical teaching should be transmitted personally and not simply through writing or academic study. In other words, it is considered to be experiential in nature. Moreover, to enable the aspirant to make progress on the mystical journey, there is a need for a teacher or shaykh. A central idea associated with a shaykh is that the tradition and teaching may be traced back ultimately to the prophet Muhammad. Another central term is that of dhikr, or remembrance of God. The key idea is always to keep the name of God within one's mind, and hence to remain focused upon devotion to God. The Sufi aspires to a gradual elimination of concerns with the material world, and an increasing concentration on the world of the spirit. The state in which there has been an elimination of concerns for the ego and self, and a concentration on God, is described as fana.

CHAPTER 6

THE NATURE MYSTICISM OF TAOISM AND SHINTO

SUMMARY

This chapter will discuss some of the common mystical threads between Taoism and Shinto, and will in particular examine the importance of the natural world within the two traditions. In the discussion of Taoism, there will be an exploration of the Taoist approach to life and existence, and among other aspects, a review of the significance of Taoism within Chinese art. In terms of Shinto, the chapter will explore the significance of shrines in natural locations, and the importance of poetry and natural beauty within the tradition. The chapter will conclude with case studies of Laozi and Matsuo Basho.

TAOISM

The Tao as described by Laozi, is the spiritual force which guides and controls the universe. Everything in the universe is perceived as being a manifestation of Tao, and existing according to the principles of Tao (see Kohn and LaFargue, 1998). One of the key features of Tao is that of harmony. The Tao ensures that all elements of the universe operate together, in a balanced, harmonious manner, and that human beings are part of this fundamental harmony. However, this harmony is not static in any sense, but rather all parts of the universe are seen as existing in a dynamic equilibrium with each other, under the general influence of the Tao. This equilibrium is in fact in a state of constant change, but that change reorientates itself through the guidance of the Tao into a new equilibrium. It is difficult to avoid an analogy here with biological theories concerning a balanced ecosystem, and the need to maintain the environment in balance and equilibrium. One might view Taoism, at least partially, as a spiritual theory which has some points of reference with contemporary ecological theory.

Taoism goes further however, in extending this general view of the mechanism of the universe, to making prescriptions about human conduct. Taking into consideration the balance of the universe, human beings should not act in a manner which is contrary to this balance. The term used in Taoism for this type of conduct is wu wei. This term describes a philosophy of action which combines an element of passivity with a degree of action. Wu wei is passive to the extent that it advocates not acting in a manner which would disrupt the Tao and the essential equilibrium of the universe. However, human beings do have to act in the world. They have to make plans, they have to act to avoid danger and to protect themselves. However, such action should not be of a kind to act against the essential principles of the Tao. Wu wei is sometimes described as 'going with the flow', and in someways that describes the philosophy very well. With wu wei one does not simply follow a course of action at any cost. A particular course of action may have adverse effects for our friends, for our surroundings or for other aspects of the world. Even if such a course of action had desirable consequences for us, it would probably be contravening the essential elements of the Tao. With wu wei one would try as far as possible to harmonize our actions with the needs of others and with the prevalent harmony of our surroundings, in their broadest sense. Importantly, we can see here the moral element within the philosophy of the Tao.

In terms then of practical action, the philosophy of wu wei encourages us to act in certain ways. It discourages us from always seeking results from what we do. For example, we will sometimes have a particular life goal in mind, and then try to do everything possible to achieve it. Sometimes this can become quite obsessive, and if we pursue it too far, it can be psychologically damaging for us. Wu wei is certainly not antagonistic to having an aim in life, as long as it does not become all-embracing. We are encouraged to do what seems natural and right, without becoming too fixed on the outcomes. It can happen that we perceive some people as acting as an obstruction to what we might like to achieve, and the result can be antagonism and mutual dislike and distrust. According to wu wei we try to act in such a way that will not result in antagonism in others. The goal is always to create harmony rather than discord.

In acting according to wu wei, it is important that we do not view the philosophy as involving passivity. Wu wei certainly involves action, but action which is in tune with the surroundings and its ultimate harmony. Practitioners of Tao would only act in a given situation when it was absolutely necessary. If it was not totally necessary then they would try to refrain from acting. Practitioners of Tao also try wherever possible to reduce their sense of egotism. Hence they try not to look out at the world from the point of view of themselves, or to assume that they have special insights into the nature of the world or of truth.

Although a Taoist view of life has elements of rationalism within it, and does not try to dissuade its followers from trying to think about problems clearly, Taoism does have a strongly intuitive element within it. Taoists would probably argue that it is not possible to understand the world completely by means of a scientific view of the world, and that we reach a point where we need to try to have an empathy with the world around us. Sometimes, this can lead us to live a less-complicated life, which is perhaps more in keeping with the Tao.

Part of this sense of empathy with the natural world involves an appreciation of the sense of duality in the world. Central to Taoism is an awareness of the opposites which exist in the world, such as light and dark, sun and shade. We would have no appreciation of sunlight, unless we also understood the nature of shade. Similarly with light and dark. This notion of complementary pairs of concepts is exemplified by the concepts of yin and yang. Yin is perceived as representing darkness, while yang represents light. These concepts however, are part of a dualistic philosophy which conceptualizes the universe as existing in a dynamic equilibrium between two forces. The yin and the yang are in a state of constant movement, at once expanding and increasing, and then diminishing, such that the overall combination remains largely constant. This notion is also a reflection of the wider functioning of the universe, where all aspects are not viewed as fixed, but as changing, adapting and evolving.

TAO TE CHING

The principal scriptural text of Taoism is the Tao Te Ching. It is normally assumed to have been written by Laozi, although there remains doubt as to whether Laozi was a single historical figure. It is generally assumed that the text was written around the fifth or sixth century BCE. The central element of the book is the concept of the Tao itself and its fundamental nature. The Tao cannot be defined or specified, but it is the eternal force which controls the universe. The text attempts to set down, within the limits of the written form, the nature of the Tao.

The Tao Te Ching weaves together a number of different concepts, but one of the principal ideas is that of the importance of softness, yielding, emptiness and flexibility, rather than hardness, rigidity and substance. In our contemporary world, we tend to admire strength and 'permanence'. We tend to admire people with 'strong' opinions, and organizations which take a firm stand on issues. We admire technological advances which appear to achieve dominance over nature, and which can create large buildings, cars or other artefacts. However, the Tao Te Ching suggests that such strength is really deceptive, and so-called permanence is really an illusion. Of the many examples or perhaps metaphors we could take, we might consider the fate of buildings in an earthquake. Very often the rigid, 'solid' buildings are destroyed because they are not constructed to move or bend with external forces. A much lighter, less-rigid structure, perhaps made of wood, will often survive the earthquake because it is flexible and able to adapt to the external forces. The walls of such a building are thin, and a much greater proportion of the construction will be empty space. With a 'solid' building, however, the walls are thick and proportionately less of the building consists of empty space. Taoism advocates the virtues of space, emptiness and adaptability. Metaphors for these qualities include wind and water. Neither of these occupy rigid space, for example. They move effortlessly adapting to the space around them. They are the very antithesis of solid structures and yet they are extremely powerful. We are only too well aware of the extent to which both can destroy so-called solid constructions.

The Tao Te Ching advocates a similar philosophical approach in relation to the way individual human beings live their lives. Taoism suggests that a continual effort to accumulate things, to gain things, to acquire material possessions, is not ultimately a satisfactory philosophy of life. The wise person, it is suggested, is one who understands the balance point at which one possesses sufficient material goods for a happy and contented life. Taoism argues in a sense, that we can live successful, happy lives with very little, and that the continual effort to accumulate things is ultimately destructive of happiness.

There is then a strong mystical element in Taoism. It is not a mysticism which involves a search for unity with a God, but rather an aspiration to live in harmony with the way in which the universe functions. Of course not all people would share the Taoist view of the world. Many, particularly in contemporary times, would probably see technological advance and 'mastery' of the natural world, as a great virtue; and one would have to agree that technology and science have brought enormous advances in the material quality of life of millions of people. Nevertheless, Taoism points to an older and more fundamental truth of the world; a truth which is fundamentally mystical, and which involves returning to our original spiritual place in the world.

This sense of balance in the world is very much reflected in the traditional systems of Chinese medicine. Philosophically, Chinese medicine has been influenced by Taoism, and within such a framework the body is seen as normally existing in equilibrium with the world surrounding it. If in any sense, this equilibrium is disturbed, then the result may well be illness, since the body cannot function well within a state of disequilibrium. When human beings are subjected to forces of imbalance external to them, such as psychological stress, this may result in illness. Different people may have the same illness or infection, but the extent to which their body systems are in imbalance may be different. The result is that within Chinese medicine, it may be necessary to treat individuals in a slightly different way, even though they have broadly the same infection.

The Taoist sense of balance in the world is again reflected in the tradition of feng shui. This is the practice of organizing and designing the physical space around human beings so that it is in harmony with nature. The philosophy of feng shui assumes that there is a natural flow of energy or qi, in the world, and that when a house or building is being constructed, it is very important to orientate it in such a way that it is in harmony with the flow of qi. It is perhaps easier to understand the philosophy of feng shui if one thinks of someone in the country, a long way from a city, planning to build a small house. It would be natural to consider the nature of the surrounding land. One might ask local people about where the water flows after heavy rain, or the direction of the wind during storms. One might look at the disposition of trees to see where the best shelter might be obtained. In short, one would plan the location of the house so that it harmonized with the local land and prevailing natural forces. The assumption would be to place the house in the best natural location, rather than assuming that a house could be constructed anywhere so long as it was built sufficiently strongly. We return here to the previous argument that Taoism encourages human beings to live in accord with nature, rather than assuming that human beings through their scientific knowledge can 'conquer' nature. We now consider another religion which is intimately connected with the natural world, and that is the Japanese religion of Shinto.

SHINTO

Unlike many religions, Shinto does not have a clear founding figure, and its origins date back to a period before written records. Nevertheless, it is an essential element in Japanese culture and has interacted with Buddhism over the years. Shinto involves more than anything else, the worship of spirits known as kami (see Littleton, 2002). Such spirits can take many different forms. Perhaps the easiest to appreciate are the kami which are supposed to reside in places of great natural beauty. Waterfalls, trees, particularly interesting stones or rock formations, hills and streams may all be thought to contain a kami specific to that location. The kami may be thought of as existing in that particular location, or it may be considered as the particular natural phenomenon itself. Other phenomena such as wind and rain may be thought to have a kami. Some kami are considered to consist of the spirits of deceased people and may become very important. Tenjin, for example, is thought to be the kami of a famous Japanese thinker and teacher, and this kami has now become very much associated with the educational process. Kami are not generally considered as deities, in the sense of the Gods of some other religions. They may be considered as, for example, sources of energy, which are part of the contemporary world. They are not in any sense separate from the everyday world in which we live. Some kami are particularly significant, for example, Amaterasu, the Goddess of the Sun.

Kami are generally worshipped at shrines, which are located close to the supposed existence of the kami. Such shrines are often very simple constructions, but it is a significant part of Japanese life to visit such shrines. The belief in kami is an example of what can be described as an animistic belief system (see Harvey, 2005). Animism is the belief that the physical world and physical objects, including living beings, are occupied by spirits. In other words, the world as we know it, including the place of human beings within it, is a spiritual place. This gives Shinto belief a very different perspective to some other religions which tend to regard the world as in various ways imperfect. Such religions tend to place an emphasis upon human beings escaping from the world because the latter is unsatisfactory. In Shinto, however, human beings are part of a world which is spiritual in nature, and the task of human beings is in a sense to affirm that spirituality rather than to escape from it. The principal ways in which this is achieved are to emphasize the role of the family and of ancestors, to affirm the commitment to the natural world and to worship kami.

Shinto manifests itself in a variety of ways in traditional Japanese culture and aesthetics. Notable is the link between Shinto beliefs and nature, and the way in which Japanese gardens are traditionally constructed. The philosophy of Shinto gardens is that they should be extremely simple in design, and should reflect the way in which plants and trees naturally grow and develop. Shinto gardens are intended to reflect nature rather than to change it. This philosophy can be contrasted with the concept of the garden in the West, where there tends to be an assumption that nature should be adapted to reflect human ideals of aesthetics. Human ideas and concepts are considered as the important starting point, and then aspects of nature in the form of specific types of plants are selected to reflect this. In the Shinto garden however, the emphasis is upon presenting nature in microcosm, as it is, rather than trying to adapt it to other values and norms. Shrines devoted to kami also reflect features of Shinto belief. Shinto emphasizes personal cleanliness as an important quality, and a shrine very often has a small building in which visitors can wash before moving on to the main shrine building.

Some would perhaps argue that Shinto is not really a religion, although this depends very much upon the criteria which one chooses to apply to the latter concept. Shinto certainly does not have a set of doctrinal beliefs, and yet at the same time it is a profoundly spiritual way of life. It embraces all aspects of life, and does provide a sense of ethics linked to the natural world. Many animistic belief systems possess the characteristic that they are all-embracing; in other words that they provide a way of living which includes all aspects of the lives of people. That seems to be reasonably close to what many would regard as a religion. Certainly, there are strong mystical elements in

Shinto. First and foremost there is the feeling of unity possessed by human beings. The individual is a part of a large and complex natural world which is fundamentally spiritual in character. The entire nature of existence is perceived as spiritual and this imbues the totality of life.

We can now consider two individuals who reflected the values of Taoism and of Shinto: Laozi and Matsuo Basho respectively.

LAOZI

Laozi is, according to tradition, the ancient sage who systematized the philosophy and practice of Taoism, and who also wrote the Tao Te Ching. He is thought to have lived in about the sixth century BCE and to have been a contemporary of Confucius. However, there is much disagreement among academics as to whether Laozi was actually a real individual, or whether he has been a useful creation during the history of Taoist culture. It may be, for example, that the Tao Te Ching was in fact written by a number of individuals, and that for convenience, the work was gradually assumed to have been written by one sage. It may be that the person of Laozi is a social construction, or it may be that he was an actual historical figure. The confirmatory evidence is simply not currently available.

According to tradition, it is thought that Laozi was responsible for the archives at the imperial court, but that in old age he decided to relinquish the post and set out on a long solitary journey towards the western border of China. It is said that a guard asked Laozi to write down his main philosophical teachings and this became the Tao Te Ching. Over the years, as his teachings gradually became better established, Laozi was regarded as a deity by some. This would not probably, however, have been highly regarded by the sage himself, who has left a subtle and complex mysticism, emphasizing the fundamental relationship between individual human beings and the natural balance and functioning of the universe.

MATSUO BASHO

Basho was one of Japan's greatest poets who wrote in the haiku tradition. Haiku are traditionally short poems of usually seventeen syllables in Japanese. Each poem is normally separated into three sections or lines. Many of Basho's poems were written during long walking journeys around Japan, and reflect the natural, unspoilt scenery of the country in the seventeenth century. Throughout their joint history in Japan, Buddhism and Shinto have interacted and combined to produce a distinctive Japanese spiritual environment, and Basho was influenced strongly by the aesthetics and spirituality of Zen and Shinto.

Matsuo Basho was born in the Japanese city of Ueno in 1644. His father was an administrator for the local ruling family, and when only a young boy, Basho also joined the service of the local feudal ruler. As he grew older he became more and more attracted to traditional Japanese art forms such as calligraphy, and particularly to literature and poetry. He gradually developed a reputation as a poet, first in Kyoto and then later in Tokyo. However, inspired by his growing sense of spirituality, he became more and more attracted to a life of meditation and quiet contemplation. It is said that a friend of his built him a modest house and that he was given a banana tree to plant in the garden of the house. This species of tree is known as a basho tree in Japanese, and it is this name which Basho decided to use, and by which he has become known.

As time progressed Basho became less and less interested in the material things of this world, and in particular in his fame as a poet, and decided to try to relinquish more and more of his possessions. This culminated in his decision at the age 40 to set out on a long journey on foot, which was a kind of personal journey or pilgrimage. During this journey he visited many shrines and temples, and recorded his feelings and impressions in haiku poems. He was to make several more lengthy journeys around Japan lasting sometimes as long as two and a half years. His journey was interspersed with periods of rest and consolidation. Finally, in 1694 CE, he died near Osaka, while on one of his long walking journeys.

Matsuo Basho had spent the final ten years of his life trying to live out the essential values of Shinto and Zen. He had relinquished his material possessions, and embarked on long journeys which continually brought him close to nature. He had meditated and reflected on how to live in harmony with the world, and used his own haiku poetry as a means of expressing his feelings about the world around him. He left a spiritual and literary legacy which is still held in high esteem in Japan.

KEY IDEAS

Taoism and Shinto share a very close affinity with nature. For both traditions, a true sense of spirituality is to be found in recognizing our closeness to and dependence upon, the natural world. It is in this commitment to exist in harmony with nature, which is at the basis of the mysticism of the two religions. The concept of wu wei in Taoism is very much linked to this respect for the natural world. The notion of action within inaction, or of adapting oneself to the natural rhythms of the world, is a complex and subtle approach. Nevertheless, it seems to be very much in accord with contemporary environmentalist ideas of acting with the living world and not against it. The related notion of yin and yang stresses the concept of equilibrium between two dissimilar forces and the idea of the universe existing in a form of dynamic stability. Equally, the importance of equilibrium in the world is also reflected in the ideas of feng shui in relation to the sense of harmony between buildings and the environment. The Tao Te Ching stresses among other concepts, the virtues of being in harmony with the flow of nature, as opposed to working against the natural world. Perhaps the central philosophical and mystical element in Shinto is that the world is conceived as a spiritual place, and that human beings, as spiritual creatures, have an important role in that world. The idea that spirit permeates all creates an atmosphere which is conducive to reflection, meditation and mystical experience.

CHAPTER 7

CHRISTIAN MYSTICISM

SUMMARY

This chapter explores the roots of Christian mysticism in the life and teachings of Jesus Christ, and of the connection between mysticism and the concept of the Holy Spirit. Techniques associated with Christian mystical practice are also discussed, including contemplation and meditation. There is an evaluation of the historical conflicts between mystical thought and Christian orthodoxy including a discussion of the Quietists and the Cathars. Case studies of two Christian mystics are provided, namely, Simone Weil and George Fox.

INTRODUCTION

Christian mysticism has a number of features in common with mysticism in other faiths, in particular in terms of the practices of prayer and self-denial which are used as part of the pathway to a deeper communion with God. Nevertheless, the unique features of Christian mysticism derive from the life of Jesus, and in particular his sacrifice on the cross for the sake of humanity. Mysticism in the Christian tradition is deeply rooted in the New Testament and in the life of Jesus as he struggled with his own mission and destiny on earth.

The mystic pathway within Christianity has traditionally been viewed in a number of different stages. The first is the practice of self-discipline. This may embrace a number of different activities, many of which would seem familiar to mystics in other traditions. Prayer is certainly one of the key elements, and is usually practised according to a preplanned structure. According to the particular tradition, certain prayers will be said at specific times of the day. The repetition and the discipline of maintaining a routine of prayer is part of the mystical training. In addition, the mystic will try to abstain from the comforts of life. Only food necessary for maintaining basic health will be consumed, and clothing will be simple and unpretentious. The mystic will also during this period try to engage in acts of charity and providing assistance for those in need. He or she will devote themselves to care for the sick and elderly, not only as a Christian pleasure and duty, but also as an element in their own spiritual progress.

This stage of mystical development will gradually evolve into one where the individual practises contemplation and meditation, reflecting upon the example of the life of Jesus, and focusing more and more upon God. The mystic will contemplate the life of Jesus, and in particular those periods when Jesus gave himself over to private prayer and reflection. During this stage of meditation, there will be a greater and greater awareness of the influence of the Holy Spirit upon the individual, who will begin to have a more and more intense vision of the nature of God. Finally, the mystic will have a closer and closer vision of God culminating in a sense of unity with the Divine. As with all mystical experience, that within Christianity is self-reported. In other words, we must rely on the reported experience of mystics to understand something of the nature of the complete experience. However, as we shall see, the accounts of different mystics, while differing sometimes in detail, do have sufficient commonality for us to suppose that the experiences are real and valid.

The mystical experience within Christianity, as it is in many ways in other religious traditions, is a process of relinquishing a hold on the world. The aspirant tries to sever the ties which have developed during a lifetime, with the material and psychological pleasures of life, and to concentrate solely on the power of the Holy Spirit, and upon God. This is never easy to achieve. The virtues of distancing oneself from the world, and the advantages of this for spiritual and mystical progress, are described, for example, in the classic work by Thomas à Kempis, *The Imitation of Christ*. The mystic may understand the necessity for this process intellectually, but achieving it may be far from easy. To try to attain this state of distancing oneself from the world, the mystic adopts a number of techniques. Central to these approaches are those of contemplation and meditation.

It is perhaps worth trying to distinguish these two terms in a conceptual sense. On the one hand, both terms can be used in an intransitive sense, to the extent that we can speak of someone 'contemplating' or 'meditating' without assuming an object of these activities. The terms can simply be used to describe a process. On the other hand, we can also speak of a person contemplating something, in the sense of there being an object of the contemplation. However, although we can speak of someone meditating 'on something', we perhaps more usually employ the word in an intransitive sense.

Contemplation has always tended to have a legitimate role within orthodox Christianity, where the object of contemplation could be a religious statue, a holy relic, a painting, or a biblical verse. One might also contemplate an abstract entity such as goodness or Christian virtue, or one might contemplate Jesus or the Virgin Mary as models of spiritual life. Christian mystics could thus practise contemplation while remaining within the parameters of mainstream Christianity. Meditation has, however, always tended to remain somewhat outside traditional Christian practice. It has tended to be regarded as too esoteric, or perhaps too typical of non-Christian faiths, to be fully embraced by Christianity. Nevertheless, meditation practice has retained a role within some Christian groups. Meditation techniques, where they are used, are fairly close to those practices used in other religions. They include breathing exercises, or repetition of spiritual phrases or mantra designed to still the mind. Sometimes prayers may be repeated over and over to try to calm the thoughts which continually arise in the mind. Overall, both contemplation and meditation are used as means of stilling the mind, detaching it from its preoccupations with the everyday world, and enabling the mystic to concentrate on God.

Central to the experience of many Christian mystics is their conceptualization of the Holy Spirit. It is in many ways rather difficult to examine this concept, since it is viewed differently by many Christian groups. Theologically, it is part of the Holy Trinity of God the Father, God the Son, and God the Holy Spirit. The problem is that different writers and different biblical texts speak of the Holy Spirit using a variety of different terminology. The Holy Spirit can be conceived first of all as a separate 'being', a part of the Trinity, having its own distinct qualities; or it can be conceived of as a spiritual force, or perhaps emanation, which reflects the power of God as demonstrated by His son Jesus. Christian mystics are more generally likely to adopt the latter position, where they would try, through the power of prayer, and through contemplation and meditation, to strengthen the power and influence of the Holy Spirit within themselves. In this way they would hope to enhance their spiritual insights and their closeness to God.

The concept of the spiritual dimension of God played a key role in one significant heterodox school of thought which was essentially mystical in nature. The Cathars were a religious group which evolved in the eleventh century in the south of France, and which developed throughout the twelfth and thirteenth centuries, eventually being destroyed in the fourteenth century. The Cathars regarded themselves as Christian, indeed as the affirmation of what was truly Christian, but their teachings were rejected by the Catholic orthodoxy, who regarded them as heretics (Lambert, 1998). Their essential world-view was dualistic, and involved the conceptual separation of the world into the material and the spiritual. The material world was regarded as fundamentally evil, while the spiritual world was essentially good. As Catholic doctrine considered the world to be the creation of God, then this immediately placed some distance between the Cathars and Catholicism.

At the heart of Cathar, mystical practice was therefore the idea of gradually relinquishing contact with the physical world. The ideal type of life was therefore one of total chastity, of not eating meat and of abstaining from alcohol, and of committing oneself to a life of prayer, reflection and helping others. This type of existence was certainly not practised by all Cathars, but in effect by a relatively small minority, who acted as exemplars for the rest of the community. The ideal type of lifestyle, if practised diligently, was supposed to help the aspirant move closer and closer to the spirit of God. It was supposed that not all people would be able to obtain a sense of mystical union with God in a single life, and hence there developed a belief in the principle of reincarnation. This doctrine was regarded by Catholic orthodoxy as a serious deviation from accepted belief, and placed the Cathars further from any possible reconciliation with Rome. Pope Innocent III established the Albigensian Crusade in 1209, to challenge and defeat the Cathars. The Pope decreed, that as part of the terms of the crusade, any lands captured in southern France, could be retained by those supporting the crusade. The result was that the nobility of northern France were very eager to join the crusade, as they saw the opportunity of extending their lands in the south. The Albigensian Crusade thus became as much the pursuit of wealth, as it did the pursuit of those defined as heretics.

The ultimate outcome of the crusade could never really have been in any doubt. Despite the apparently impregnable castles in the Aude region of France, which sheltered the Cathar communities, there was no means by which they could resist the formidable military forces ranged against them. Over a period of about a century, aided later by the Inquisition, the Cathar faith was gradually eliminated or absorbed into orthodox Catholicism. The suppression of the Cathar faith was brutal in the extreme, even by the standards of medieval Europe. However, in the history of religions across the world, it often appears that the severest punishments have been reserved for those who attempted to adapt belief systems and move them too far from the agreed orthodoxy. A similar fate befell the medieval Spanish mystic, Saint John of the Cross who was tortured, but later managed to resume his religious activities. He is particularly well known for writing the classic text, the *Dark Night of the Soul*, which outlines the journey of the soul towards union with God. A text on the same subject was written by Saint John's spiritual colleague, Saint Teresa of Avila.

A central theme in the history of Christian mysticism has been that of trying to emulate the mystical experiences of Jesus Christ. There is however a fundamental difference between trying to replicate say the enlightenment experiences of the historical Buddha, and trying to replicate the mystical experiences of Jesus. In the case of the Buddha there was no theological dimension to his existence or to his teaching. He perceived himself, and was perceived by others, as an ordinary man. Although we may think of him as being particularly spiritually advanced, there is no logical reason why someone else should not, given due diligence and effort, replicate the enlightenment of the historical Buddha. The case of Jesus is, however, rather different. Although he assumed human form, he is conceptualized as part of the Holy Trinity, and as possessing an element of the Divine within him. We might reasonably suppose that his relationship with God was qualitatively different from that which is possible for ordinary human beings. Christian mystics may attempt to replicate the practices of Jesus, to pray in the same way, and to contemplate God in the same way, but it is at least questionable whether a sense of mystical union with God is the same as that possible for Jesus Christ.

Christian mystics, as is the case in many other religious traditions, have often found great difficulty in putting their spiritual experiences into words. Perhaps the commonest strategy has been that of the use of metaphorical language, drawing an analogy between heightened spiritual awareness, and more everyday occurrences. The union of the human soul with God, for example, has been compared with the marriage of a man and woman. The points of comparison include the profound sense of love, the sheer emotional intensity of the feelings between husband and wife, and the sense of commitment. One might also point to differences, however. The marriage of two people on earth is ultimately destined for separation through death, while the union of the soul with God may continue for eternity.

The language of religious experience and in particular descriptions of mystical feeling have often historically been at the heart of conflict between mystics and the established religious authorities. In medieval Europe, the Catholic Church was arguably the single most important unifying force in society. Its power and influence transcended the boundaries of nation-states, and its authority was equally important in both a religious sense and also in the secular realms of society, as a political force. In the latter sense, it could also exercise important power, through its ability to legitimize war and conquest. The effective exercise of this power could only take place if there was no significant challenge to the religious doctrine of the Catholic Church. Any challenge to the fundamental teachings undermined its position as the sole interpreter of God's will on earth. Of all the groups who could potentially challenge the Church, mystics of various persuasions were perhaps the most significant. Whatever, the specific belief system of different mystics, their general emphasis upon the importance of individual spiritual experience, at the expense of the collective, was always a potential challenge to the Church. In the most extreme cases, there was a rejection by mystics of the entire purpose and justification of the Church. The argument was that the mystic related directly with God and hence any earthly social structure was entirely superfluous. In such cases, the mystic could argue that the entire structure of Christian ceremony and ritual was unnecessary to the single purpose of achieving a direct and personal relationship with God.

The so-called Quietist movement, which was influential in mainland Europe in the seventeenth century, emphasized this personal relationship with God. The aim of Quietist mystics was to establish this close relationship with God, and then to ensure that this relationship permeated all aspects of their lives. The Quietist attempted to live every moment thinking and reflecting upon God. In so doing, Quietists arrived at a position where they ceased completely to think about themselves. The 'I' ceased to exist, and they became focused solely upon God. This abandonment of 'self' also affected the manner in which Quietists prayed. They tended not to ask for God's intervention in the world. Prayer was devotional rather than supplicatory. For the Quietists it did not appear logical or indeed perhaps ethical, to ask God to favour them in someway, when their whole philosophical approach was to try to eliminate the notion of the self.

The denial of the ego or self has been a repeated theme throughout the history of mysticism and indeed appears in a number of traditions. Perhaps the most well known is in Buddhism, where the concept of 'no-self' is a central element in Buddhist philosophy. A celebrated medieval German philosopher and theologian, Meister Eckhart, who is thought to have died in 1328 CE, was another mystic who argued strongly for the elimination of ideas of the self (Tobin, 1986). Condemned during his lifetime as a heretic, his work has become popular in contemporary times, and is regularly discussed in relation to similarities with Eastern mysticism.

GEORGE FOX

George Fox was born in 1624 and was the moving force behind the establishment of the Quaker movement, or Religious Society of Friends. He was born in Leicestershire in the town of Fenny Drayton, into a fairly wealthy family. His father was a successful weaver and the family life was comfortable financially. When he was about 11 years of age he became an apprentice to a local shoemaker. However, in his late teens, he appears to have become more and more unsettled and dissatisfied with his life. He abandoned his apprenticeship and went to live in London for about a year, before returning home. There is no doubt that at this time, George was very interested in spiritual matters. He embarked on a series of travels around the middle counties of England, where partly through debate with others and partly through personal reflection he attempted to resolve some of his own spiritual dilemmas. He was clearly going through a period when he was suffering many personal anxieties and was trying to find a means of resolving these. He also was becoming gradually alienated from the hierarchical system of the Church, and the degree of power and authority exercised by parish clergy.

In 1647 Fox appears to have experienced a profound spiritual revelation during which he came to believe that Jesus Christ could resolve his spiritual problems, and that Jesus could communicate directly with him in a spiritual sense. George came to the conclusion that ultimately neither an external person such as a priest was necessary for this spiritual communion, nor were even scriptures essential. Fundamentally, what was required was an internal spiritual voice speaking directly from Jesus. The general trend of his thinking was away from a commitment to the orthodoxy of the Church and a move in the direction of individual spirituality. One of the consequences of this was a predictable antagonism on the part of the Church, but also it did lead to a situation where there were a number of different viewpoints and perspectives within Fox's movement. It was difficult to advocate individual spirituality, without engendering a diversity of belief within the movement.

George Fox travelled across the Midlands and then into Yorkshire. He was imprisoned for a time at Derby, since his teachings were tending to be regarded as potentially disruptive (Ingle, 1994). He was very much against the prevailing principle that only well-educated people could in effect say anything worthwhile about God and religion. At his meetings, all people of whatever social class or gender were encouraged to speak. His movement could then be regarded as having some socialist tendencies, and was certainly a challenge to the established social order. He made speeches and gained many converts around the area between the north Yorkshire Dales and the Lake District. One follower was Margaret Fell, and Fox was later a guest a Swarthmoor Hall, the home of Margaret and Thomas Fell. The latter was an influential figure holding the post of vice-chancellor of the Duchy of Lancaster. Thomas Fell, who was also a judge, was able to exert some influence on behalf of Fox, when he found himself in trouble with the legal authorities, as he did from time to time. As the movement developed, it began to develop the rudiments of an administrative structure. The occasional private religious meetings were gradually being replaced by regular meetings, where some administrative decisions were taken. In addition some of the essential teachings of the movement were being increasingly written down in pamphlets and booklets, and being distributed in major cities, accompanied by the efforts of Quaker missionaries. Fox later travelled to London, and managed to obtain a meeting with Oliver Cromwell, who although somewhat suspicious of his teachings and actions gave him qualified support.

In 1660, with the restoration of the monarchy, there was increased antagonism towards the rather radical message of the Quakers. They were viewed by the government as a potential source of subversion. Partly as a moral and religious statement, but also perhaps designed to minimize the antagonism towards Quakers, Fox wrote a pamphlet in which he declared that the movement was completely against any form of participation in physical violence or warfare. This did not, however, reduce the level of suspicion in the government, and an act was passed making it illegal to hold a religious gathering of more than five people, for any denomination or sect different to the Church of England. In addition, there was an increasing number of arrests of Quakers across the country and many found themselves in prison. There was also considerable dissent within the movement over a variety of issues. Essentially it derived from the philosophical issue of individual viewpoints within a democratic movement. There was so much diversity of view that it was not easy to ensure some form of cohesion.

By 1669, Margaret Fell was a widow, and she and George Fox decided to marry. Margaret continued her active work for the movement and was afterwards imprisoned for her activities. In 1671, Fox decided to visit the quite large Quaker community in Barbados. While there he encouraged slaves to attend Quaker meetings. He then travelled to Jamaica and up the east coast of America, where many Quaker communities were well established. He generally received a warm welcome. On returning to England, a number of long-standing disputes continued, notably one concerning the equality of women within Quakerism and their right to hold their own women's meetings. In the coming years he worked on his Journal, or in effect his autobiography. In 1691, while still deeply engaged in Quaker business, he died in London. Quite apart from his achievement in establishing the Quaker movement, he articulated the importance of the internal voice of God within the individual and the mystical experiences ensuing from that.

SIMONE WEIL

Simone Weil was in many ways one of the most remarkable intellectuals of the twentieth century. She was at the same time philosopher, religious thinker, mystic and social reformer. She was born in Paris in 1909 to Jewish parents who largely did not practise their faith. Her father was a doctor. Both parents were well educated with wide-ranging interests, and they encouraged their children to work very hard at their education. It was evident from an early age that both Simone and her brother Andre were extremely talented. Andre was a mathematical prodigy, while Simone learned several foreign languages at a young age. Simone studied at several leading lycées in Paris, and obtained her baccalaureate in 1925. She then became a student at the highly academic Lycée Henri IV, where she studied under the philosopher Emile-Auguste Chartier, who was a considerable influence upon her academic development. It was at this period that Simone published her writing for the first time, and Chartier aided her in this. In 1928, she was offered a place at the Ecole Normale Superieure. She then obtained her aggregation in philosophy in 1931. Simone tended to give little attention to her dress and appearance, and this perhaps added to her reputation of being rather eccentric. She was beginning to develop a philosophy at this time that it was undesirable to be too attached to the results of one's work, and that one should simply work without any particular regard for the consequences. Later in her life, when she read the Bhagavad Gita, and began studies in Sanskrit, she would have come across a related version of this philosophy.

After graduating she taught philosophy in a series of lycées, but appears not to have settled very well into the role of teacher. She does not seem to have got on very well with her colleagues in general, and the number of times she changed teaching posts suggests that she may not have been entirely happy in the role. During this time she increasingly became involved in a role as social activist. She cultivated the acquaintance of workers in manual jobs, and in many cases arranged to work alongside them to learn something of their lives, difficulties and world-view. She participated in marches and demonstrations to protest about wages and working conditions for workers, and at one stage in 1934 worked for a time in a Renault car plant, on the production line. She found this work very hard physically, but appeared pleased that she was able to learn something of the lives of the working classes. Simone had a clear concept of the role of the intellectual and academic in society. She considered that it was inappropriate for an intellectual to remain isolated from life, and that the best role was to be thoroughly involved in life's challenges, and contribute something to the lives of others in society. She felt this was particularly so for those in poorly paid and difficult jobs. In 1936, she was a volunteer on the Republican side in the Spanish Civil War, but found the harsh environment extremely difficult. It was during this period that she met Trotsky. She continued to study a wide range of subjects, and read extensively in the area of religion. In 1937, she travelled to Assisi in Italy, and visited the Church where St Francis prayed. This visit appears to have had a significant effect upon her spiritual life. Simone had suffered debilitating headaches and migraines for most of her adult life, and these had become so bad at this period that she decided gradually to abandon her teaching career. She started to read Hindu scriptures, and became more and more interested in the spiritual dimension to life. Although very drawn to Christianity, she was by nature unattracted by the idea of joining organizations, or of submitting herself to a complete ideology or belief system of the world. Nevertheless, she began more and more to interpret the world within a spiritual and mystical framework (McLellan, 1990). Although very interested in the full range of world religions and in the variety of spiritual experience, she was not in favour of combining the different religions into an overarching idea of religious experience. She considered that each faith had its own distinctive qualities, and demonstrated its own sense of truth independently of other religions.

At the start of the Second World War she had to leave France because of her Jewish origins. She entrusted the large part of her writing to a friend, and left for the United States along with her parents. She then came to England and obtained work with General De Gaulle's government in exile in London. She was, however, profoundly disturbed by the conditions under which French people were living in occupied France, and this led her to limit her food intake, for example, as a mark of solidarity with the people in France. She appeared to experience a form of spiritual and mystical unity with her fellow citizens, and with their suffering. She may have felt a kind of spiritual responsibility to suffer herself in the same way. The result was that she did not care for herself as well as she might, and her health and perhaps mental condition gradually declined. She died in Ashford in Kent in 1943.

KEY IDEAS

The concept of Christian mysticism is analysed in terms of the life of Jesus and the influence of the Holy Spirit. The ideas of contemplation and meditation are discussed and compared. The two concepts have a long history in the context of Christian mysticism, and Christian orthodoxy has tended to take slightly different views about the terms. The idea of heresy is explored in terms of the historical conflicts between mystical thought and traditional theological teachings. Christian mystical thought is wide-ranging, and case study examples are drawn from the lives of George Fox and Simone Weil.

CHAPTER 8

KABBALAH

SUMMARY

This chapter discusses the origins of Kabbalah or Jewish mystical thought, and relates it to the revelation of Moses on Mount Sinai. It explores the key writings of Kabbalah and its main concepts, and examines how these mystical ideas came to influence mainstream Judaic thought. The chapter analyses the connection between Hasidism and Kabbalah, and examines the lives and contribution of two key kabbalistic thinkers, Isaac Luria and Yehuda Ashlag.

INTRODUCTION

The Kabbalah is a tradition and body of knowledge which is usually described in contemporary times as 'Jewish mysticism'. There is certainly a large body of writing within Judaism which is esoteric, complex, and no doubt very difficult for the orthodox practitioner to follow. As this developed over the centuries, it was not regarded particularly as 'mystical' but often as an outcome of study and reflection upon the scriptures. As with mystical traditions in many other faiths, the term 'mystical' has tended to be appended later, to try to distinguish Kabbalah from other aspects of Judaism.

The term Kabbalah carries connotations of that knowledge which has been received or passed down. Ultimately this refers to the revelation of the Torah received by Moses directly from God. This immediately suggests one of the apparent contradictions of the Kabbalah. In placing such an emphasis upon revelation, it marks out the Kabbalah as being in at least one sense, a part of orthodox tradition. It does not assume as its starting point, scriptures or texts which are unorthodox, but rather those which are part of the mainstream.

In many mystical traditions there is an emphasis upon the individual withdrawing from the accepted, orthodox tradition and developing original insights. Some of this mystical knowledge may be very different from the accepted tradition. The source of such mystical knowledge is very often perceived as the individual mystic developing a new relationship with the Divine, or with a spiritual entity in the universe. The emphasis is usually upon individual effort through prayer, meditation or ascetic practices. Such mystical insights may depend very little upon traditional scriptures or writings, but create a new way of regarding the spiritual world. Within kabbalistic thought however, there has been a traditional emphasis upon mystical knowledge as being derived from the study of traditional scripture. In other words, the mystical element is present in scripture, as revealed to Moses on Mount Sinai, and the mystic can locate this with careful reading of scripture. The mystic is thus perceived less as an individual seeker treading a solitary and unique path towards mystical understanding, but more as a careful and meticulous student who seeks to expose the mystical and spiritual content in traditional scripture. At various times, particularly throughout the Middle Ages, for example, different groups of kabbalists made claims to the discovery of new mystical teachings in the scriptures.

The perceptions of the Kabbalah within Judaism vary somewhat. On the one hand, there are those who view it as an important analysis of traditional scripture, and hence central to Jewish belief. On the other hand, some see it as at best marginal to the faith, and at worst a heresy. Perhaps one of the causes of this range of views is the very diversity of kabbalistic thought itself. At various times kabbalists have ventured into metaphysics, astrology and magic, and have suggested very unusual and unorthodox interpretations of the world, which are difficult to place on any rational basis. The result is that it is difficult to summarize kabbalistic thought in a few concise principles. Its very variety results in appeal for some and rejection by others. It is also perhaps a truism that with extremely diverse systems of thought, individual followers can see in it what they will and this itself leads to even greater diversity.

One concept which is certainly shared between Kabbalah and orthodox Judaism is the importance of God. Everything in the universe is considered to be the creation of a single monotheistic God. Kabbalists, however, distinguish between two different facets of God. First there is an element of God and of God's power which is fundamentally beyond the perception of mere human beings. This transcendent aspect of God is a reflection of His supreme power and authority, which is conceived as so vast that it is beyond the conception of man. Secondly, there is a more imminent facet of God, which reflects His capacity to interact with man and the world. An important concept within this imminent aspect is the *sephirot* (Leaman, 2006: 93). As part of this concept God is thought of as having ten aspects which are used in the creation process and which can be at least partially perceived by human beings. God is seen as having the power to use these aspects of Himself for the continual improvement of the human condition, but can withdraw his intervention if human beings are not acting in an ethical manner. For example, if human society starts to act in unethical ways, then God can withdraw different facets of the sephirot, and not intervene to help human beings.

THE TORAH

The Torah is arguably the starting point of kabbalistic thought. It contains the first five books of the Jewish Bible and is often referred to as the *Pentateuch*. The five books are Genesis, Exodus, Leviticus, Numbers and Deuteronomy. The Torah is normally thought of as having been revealed by God to Moses on Mount Sinai. One may hypothesize whether the Torah was directly dictated to Moses, or whether Moses wrote it under a form of divine inspiration. Nevertheless, this is seen as the origin of the Torah. It is perhaps the central element of the synagogue, and of the Jewish community, particularly when in the form of a handwritten scroll.

However, the Torah was not absolutely precise about a range of Jewish customs and instructions for living, and hence a degree of interpretation became necessary. This analysis and interpretation of the Torah became what is known as the Oral Law, simply because it was originally passed on from generation to generation, entirely orally. Eventually the Jewish community came to the conclusion that the Oral Law would need to be in written form, and this was accomplished in the second century CE, resulting in the *Mishnah*. The latter was supplemented by later analyses and interpretations carried out in Babylon and Jerusalem, the entire work then being known as the *Talmud* (Rosen, 2003: 51). Much Jewish mystical writing and thought starts with the Torah, and arguably the most important kabbalistic work, the Zohar, is essentially a commentary upon the Torah.

ZOHAR

The Zohar is not simply one book but in fact a collection of works some written in Aramaic and some in Hebrew. A central part of the collection consists of an analysis of the first five books of the Hebrew Bible, but there are also discussions of the nature of the human soul and of God, and an analysis of the process of creation. In addition, there are sections concerning the nature of good and evil. There is a debate about the origin and authorship of the Zohar. The book apparently first appeared in Spain in the Middle Ages, but is written in such a way as to imply that it was actually composed by much earlier prophets and thinkers in about the second century CE. The language of the Zohar is also extremely complex and unusual. Moses de Leon who first published the book claimed that it had indeed been written by much earlier mystics.

The Zohar is today regarded as a very important book within orthodox Judaism, and it is broadly accepted that it was written during the suggested earlier period, and not by de Leon himself. However, there are many competing views. Some suggest that the works were transmitted orally for many centuries and finally committed to writing by de Leon. Others suggest that de Leon and other mystics collaborated in its creation. The issue of authorship may never be finally settled.

Central to the theology of the Zohar is a concept of God, as a very complex entity, made up of many different facets including two opposing elements which may be conceptualized as male and female. This contrasts clearly with the more singular, straightforward view of God within Jewish orthodoxy. The Zohar is also characterized by a view of phenomena in the world as being composed of two elements, an exoteric element and an esoteric element. The esoteric aspects of the empirical world enable mystics to begin to understand something of a hidden mystical world within Judaism. Many parts of the Zohar consist of an analysis of different biblical verses, and these analyses are so complex, and also presented in such an unstructured manner, that it can be difficult to appreciate an overall system to the book. The Zohar placed great emphasis upon personal religious experience including in particular the act of prayer. The book to some extent challenges the practices of traditional Judaism, releasing the process of prayer from its place in orthodox practice, and emphasizing its role in helping the individual mystic to achieve a close and personal understanding of God.

The Zohar also contains many themes which are cosmological in nature. For instance, it discusses at length, the emergence of the sephirot from God, and its employment in the creation of the universe. The latter is also linked very closely with the nature of Jewish social and community life, its structures, customs and ethics. In this way there is a kind of link between the Jewish traditional lifestyle and the process whereby God, through the sefirot, has created the universe. Moreover, the Zohar describes the process whereby God influences the world. The Zohar conceives of the existence of a spiritual flow of energy from God to human beings. When humans behave in a moral and ethical manner, and when their behaviour conforms to Jewish principles, then the flow of spiritual energy increases. Conversely when the Jewish people tend to behave in an unethical manner then the flow of spiritual energy is diminished.

OTHER WORKS OF JEWISH MYSTICISM

The Sefer Yetzirah is a kabbalistic work whose origins are subject to some debate. It is traditionally believed that it contains mystical insights revealed directly to Abraham, although some scholars believe the work to be of medieval origin. The work contains interesting moral theories about the relationship between human beings, the natural world and the physical universe. The ethics of the Sefer Yetzirah encapsulate a form of moral relativism. Every aspect of the universe exists also as its polar opposite. Beauty and ugliness exist together as opposites, as do peace and war. The ethical hypothesis is that there is nothing fundamentally unethical about any of these opposites in the universe. Rather they are evaluated purely in terms of their impact upon human beings. However, human beings are viewed as possessing an independence of thought and action, and hence may respond to these opposites in different ways. In terms of peace and war for example, one individual may be inspired to adopt a very peaceful, spiritual existence, while another may take the decision to become aggressive and belligerent. Those people, who respond positively to the opposites, have the opportunity to live in harmony with nature, while others may not have that opportunity. This is clearly a moral system which depends less upon adherence to externally imposed norms of behaviour, but much more upon independent analysis of moral issues and the concept of free will.

Another important kabbalistic work is the book Bahir, which is normally attributed to Isaac the Blind, and published in France during the medieval era. However, it is also asserted that parts of the work have a much earlier origin. This work is particularly interesting as the concept of the sephirot is first introduced here.

HASIDISM

Hasidism is a movement within Judaism which has a number of interconnections with Kabbalah. Hasidism developed in Poland and Eastern Europe in the eighteenth century, and the founder is normally considered to have been Israel ben Eliezer, who was known as the Baal Shem Tov (Shokek, 2001: 49). This latter title was usually shortened to the Besht. During this period in Eastern Europe, the Jewish community had become to some extent disenchanted with traditional Judaism, and particularly with its scholastic tendencies. The Besht advocated an approach to religion which placed emphasis upon a direct love for God, and of respect and care for other human beings. The straightforward nature of this approach to religion had a great appeal for many Jews, and the Hasidic movement spread rapidly. The appeal of Hasidism was at least partly because of its emphasis on a sense of happiness when involved in prayer and worship, but also because the approach of the Besht spoke to the needs of both academic, scholarly Jews, and also those with a more everyday approach to their religion.

On the death of the Besht, one of his disciples Rabbi Dov Ber took over the leadership of the movement. Hasidism spread throughout much of Eastern Europe and much later the ideas were taken to Western Europe and to the United States. Hasidism has within it a strongly panentheistic element, in that God is perceived as both all-powerful and present in all things in the universe. The philosophic position taken therefore by Hasidic Judaism is that if God is present in all human beings and in all aspects of the physical universe, then all daily activities and all interactions with other living things are in effect interactions with God. The implications of this philosophical position are clearly very broad. The way, any manner, in which a person acts is a form of communication with God. If God is in all individuals, when two people interact, then there is a form of two-way communication with God. God influences the individual, and the individual human being can have an influence on God.

This philosophical position leads logically to an emphasis upon the practical in religion. Everyday life can be an arena in which the individual responds to the divine presence in everything.

Hasidism extends its philosophical position of adopting a simple, uncomplicated approach to religious practice, to the esoteric complexities of Kabbalah. It asserts that it is possible in principle to reduce these complexities to straightforward conceptions of spirituality, which can be understood by anyone. Prayer, for example, is regarded as an essential element of Hasidic practice. Hasidic Jews are often noted for their characteristic attire, and some aspects of this reflect the mysticism which is intrinsic to their belief system (Cohn-Sherbok, 1997: 27). Some Hasidic men wear a shiny overcoat made of silk or satin, which is said to be a metaphor for the idea within Kabbalah of being enveloped within a shining, divine light.

ISAAC LURIA

Arguably one of the leading exponents and advocates of kabbalistic thought throughout the centuries was Isaac Luria. He was born in 1534 CE in Jerusalem, and he died in 1572 CE in Safed, Palestine. As a boy, Luria was brought up by relatives in Cairo, and there received a very thorough Jewish education. In his early twenties he became extremely interested in mysticism and decided to adopt a mendicant lifestyle, living in seclusion on a small island in the River Nile, so that he could pray and meditate in peace. He visited his family on the Sabbath, but apart from this maintained the lifestyle of a religious mendicant for six or seven years. During this period, Luria is reputed to have communicated with the prophet Elijah, and to have received advice to move to Safed to pursue his religious lifestyle. Hence in 1569, Luria moved to Palestine, to a location which was already developing a reputation as a place of religious thought and practice.

Safed had gradually developed as a place of religious study, primarily as a consequence of the expulsion of the Jewish community from Spain in 1492. The latter event must have been extremely traumatic for a community which was well established, and thriving both economically and intellectually. Nevertheless it was immediately necessary for the community to find places of refuge where new communities and centres of learning could be established. These were found in one or two places in Europe and also in Turkey. Another main centre was at Safed, which became famous as a centre of kabbalistic study including the Zohar. Moses Cordovero authored a significant analysis of the Zohar at Safed, and another leading Jewish thinker, Joseph Caro, wrote a key text on Jewish law. Isaac Luria thus arrived at a town which was well established as a place of Jewish thought and writing.

Unfortunately Isaac Luria was only to live approximately two years at Safed before his early death. During this period however, he had a very great impact on Judaic thought, and particularly in relation to the Kabbalah. One of his first actions was to gather around him a group of like-minded thinkers including Cordovero and Caro. The group, which included both relative newcomers to kabbalistic discourse, and experienced thinkers, met once a week to exchange ideas and discuss areas of interest. One of Luria's main collaborators was Rabbi Chaim Vital, with whom he spent a great deal of time, and who transcribed much of Luria's teachings. Vital also passed on some of these teachings to others. Luria also wrote a number of very celebrated mystical poems. Gradually his teachings became both widely disseminated and accepted as a significant aspect of Judaic thought. By about 50 years after his death, his ideas were becoming slowly accepted as a part of mainstream Judaic teaching. The expulsion from Spain had had a widespread effect upon the Jewish community throughout the Mediterranean area, and a key element of Luria's teachings addressed the question of how human beings could make sense of such terrible events in their lives.

At the very heart of the teachings of Luria is an account of God's creation of the world and of the part which mankind should subsequently play in the world. God is, according to Luria, entirely infinite. However, to create the universe and human beings, God needed to create some space within His infinite extension. He achieved this by partially withdrawing into Himself, and creating a form of vacuum in which the creative process could take place. Once He created the space in which He could act, He then generated a very powerful divine light focused on this created space.

Within this divine space were conceived ten vessels which collectively were known as the sephirot. These ten vessels can be thought of a means by which God can interact with mankind, and indeed these ten vessels or facets of God are considered to be partially perceived by human beings. However, within this metaphysical system of Luria, while the three upper vessels could withstand the force of the divine stream of light, the seven lower vessels were incapable of doing so, and hence broke. On the one hand, the three upper vessels were thought of as a metaphor for those aspects of the universe which had supported the notion of creation, and hence were considered to be moral and ethical. On the other hand, the seven lower vessels were a metaphor for those aspects of the universe which had been opposed to the act of creation, and hence represented evil in the world, and those forces which did not wish mankind to progress. This shattering (or *shevirah*) of the lower seven vessels, thus came to represent in a mystical, metaphorical way the difference between good and evil in the world.

But that is not the end of this symbolic story. The key aspect is the way in which mankind is now given the task of repairing the world (or *tikkun olam*). This process is essentially an ethical one, which involves every Jewish person ensuring as far as possible that they dutifully keep the law and commandments. Each time they do this, according to the metaphor of Luria, a fragment of the divine light is returned from the shattered lower vessels of the sephirot to the unbroken upper vessels. Conversely, on each occasion that someone acts unethically or not in accord with the commandments, then the existence of evil in the world is sustained by the residual existence of divine light in the lower vessels. The Lurianic philosophy thus places a kind of moral imperative upon all members of the Jewish community to act in such a way as to redeem the world. Eventually, if all members of the community act in unison, all fragments of the divine light will be returned to the upper vessels, and there will no longer be any energy to sustain evil in the world.

The theory of creation developed by Isaac Luria was thus a very complex symbolic, metaphysical system, full of obscure kabbalistic ideas. At the same time, it was also very orthodox, exhorting ordinary Jews to do their utmost to fulfil the commandments. Perhaps it was this diversity of approach which led to the wide appeal of Luria's ideas, and the interest they raised across the spectrum of Jewish thought and practice (De Lange, 2003: 100).

YEHUDA ASHLAG

Rabbi Yehuda Ashlag was a celebrated kabbalist teacher who was born in Poland in 1885, and who died in Israel in 1954. He was also known by the name Baal HaSulam or Master of the Ladder, since he wrote a very famous analysis of the Zohar, which was called Sulam or ladder.

When he was young, Ashlag was an extremely diligent student of the Torah and also of kabbalist texts. He gained the title of Rabbi in Warsaw when he was 19 years old, and continued to teach and study. At this time, he also studied the work of Karl Marx, an intellectual background which was to influence his important social philosophy when he lived and worked in Israel. During this period in Warsaw, there is a well-known story that he met a devout and knowledgeable practitioner of Kabbalah, who taught him for a period of time. There was a temporary break between Ashlag and his teacher, but the relationship was renewed and the teacher, according to the story, transmitted some special, esoteric Kabbalah teaching to Ashlag. Unfortunately, so it is said, the teacher unfortunately died the day afterwards. To this day, neither the identity of the kabbalist teacher, nor the specific nature of the mystical teachings are known.

In 1921, Ashlag decided to move to Palestine and settled there with his family. Three years later he was given a post of Rabbi at Jerusalem. After a brief period in London, Ashlag and his family returned to Palestine and moved to Jaffa. It was during this period of his life that he wrote the Talmud Eser Sefirot. This was his detailed discussion of the work of Luria including an analysis of Luria's theory of creation. Perhaps the most significant feature of Ashlag's work was that he sought to disseminate kabbalistic knowledge as widely as possible. Throughout the history of Kabbalah, there had always been a sense in which it was regarded as esoteric knowledge, suitable only for those who embarked on a serious study of its intricacies. Ashlag took a very different viewpoint, arguing that ordinary people could benefit from its teachings, and perhaps moreover, that he had a responsibility to spread that understanding. He particularly felt that the kabbalistic teachings could help human beings overcome tendencies towards self-centredness, which he considered to be at the heart of many of the social problems of the day.

Although the term Kabbalah carries connotations of 'receiving' knowledge and wisdom, Ashlag tried to transform this philosophical basis. He argued that the essence of Kabbalah should be to give to one's fellow human beings, rather than to receive something from them. In other words, one of the key benefits of kabbalistic philo-sophy was to help people develop a social philosophy of turning outwards towards other human beings, instead of turning inwards towards the self. In Ashlag's view, this philosophy should not remain simply a philosophy, but should be reflected in the political and economic organization of society, so that human beings could live according to kabbalistic teachings, within a fairer and more egalitarian society.

KEY IDEAS

The word Kabbalah signifies 'receiving', in the sense of receiving a mystical, rather esoteric knowledge of God. This knowledge is assumed to originate in God's revelation to Moses on Mount Sinai. On the one hand, kabbalistic practice has always tended to preserve its knowledge as rather secret and only for the initiated. This has been reflected in the complex style in which kabbalistic ideas have been recorded in writing. On the other hand, much kabbalistic practice has stressed the importance of maintaining the orthodox practices of Judaism. In contemporary times, there have been arguments for the democratization of kabbalistic knowledge, notably by Yehuda Ashlag.

CHAPTER 9

HINDU MYSTICISM

SUMMARY

This chapter examines the nature of mysticism within Hinduism, a religion which, by its very nature, can be viewed as fundamentally mystical. The chapter explores a central idea of Hinduism, that of the individual human being aspiring to unite with the spiritual force or divinity governing the universe. This idea is explored through scriptures such as the Upanishads. There is also a discussion of the characteristics of the mystic, and the nature of the mystical life. This is analysed in terms of the Bhagavad Gita, and through a discussion of the lives of several different Hindu mystics. The bhakti tradition of Hinduism is also discussed. There is finally a discussion of yoga, and the variety of philosophies and practices embraced within this term.

INTRODUCTION

Hinduism is characterized by a diversity of religious practice and belief, to such an extent that it is extremely difficult to encapsulate the essence of the religion by pointing to a few distinct characteristics. However, in trying to make sense of this diversity, and specifically in trying to clarify the mystical facets of the religion, one has to generalize to avoid the danger of becoming enmeshed in detail. A recurring theme within Hinduism is that of the relationship between the soul of the individual person and the 'universal soul' of the spiritual force which is seen as the source of creation (Avari, 2007). This relationship is perhaps articulated best in the scriptures known as the Upanishads.

These scriptures date from approximately fifth century BCE, and constitute the final portion of the Vedas. They are consequently often referred to as the Vedanta. The term Upanishads is often considered to derive from a Sanskrit root meaning 'to sit next to'. This connotes the idea of the disciple sitting next to the guru, and receiving spiritual wisdom. The content of the Upanishads is philosophical, dealing with many complex issues including the relationship between the individual and the Absolute. They are written in a very varied style, the content ranging from religious aphorisms and argument, to stories designed to illustrate a particular spiritual teaching. The Upanishads may originally have been written for those who had progressed in years beyond the householder stage of life, and were beginning to consider those complex questions concerning the nature of existence. At any rate, these scriptures have found a central place in Hindu philosophical teaching, and are turned to by Hindus seeking inspiration or an understanding of the place of the human being in the universe. They also offer a hypothetical solution to one of the fundamental dilemmas of the Hindu, that of karma and rebirth.

Within Hinduism, there is the belief that the existence in which a human being finds himself or herself is not the first existence to be experienced and will not normally be the last. In other words, human beings are reborn many times, and consequently suffer the pain and hardship associated with those lives. The key factor in determining the type of new existence into which people are born is the way in which they have conducted themselves in previous lives. If they have conducted themselves well, according to accepted moral norms, then they will normally benefit from a very positive rebirth. However, immoral deeds in the past will have an adverse effect on future rebirths. In addition, the manner in which we live our current life, will seriously affect our new incarnation once this life is over (Michaels, 2004). Hindus view this apparently endless sequence of death and rebirth as being highly undesirable, and will strive to escape from this cycle of events. Obtaining release from this cycle is known as '*moksha*'.

The Upanishads propose a means of attaining 'moksha', through achieving the union of the individual with Brahman, the spiritual force which creates and supports all of existence. Within the Upanishadic system of thought, the individual human being is considered to have a soul, the atman. At the same time, there is what we might consider to be a 'universal' soul, Brahman. The latter is extremely difficult to define. In fact, it is considered impossible, in a sense, to 'define' Brahman by reference to anything else. In other words, by the very concept of Brahman, it is impossible to describe this universal soul, using descriptors taken from the empirical world. Brahman is seen as having no form, or visible characteristics, yet the power and potential of Brahman extends to infinity. Brahman has the capacity to generate all aspects of the phenomena of the world which we can see and touch, whether human or of the material, physical world. As Brahman has created all of humanity, Brahman is by definition present in the individual atman. However, because human beings live in the empirical world, and are often preoccupied with everyday material concerns, they may not realize that through having that element of Brahman within them, they have the possibility of union with Brahman, thus escaping from the cycle of birth and death. This divine union, and the obtaining of moksha, is at the heart of the mysticism of the Upanishads.

ADVAITA

The philosophy of advaita derives from the Upanishads, and is usually translated as 'non-dualism'. Essentially this reflects the view that there is no fundamental distinction between the individual soul and the universal soul of Brahman. The philosophy of advaita was originally stated in a precise form by the philosopher, teacher and mystic, Sankara, in the eighth century CE. The life of Sankara will be explored later in the chapter, but here we will summarize briefly his essential teaching. The non-separation between the individual and Brahman does raise a question about the nature of the empirical world. Some critics of advaita have suggested that the philosophy is really arguing that the empirical world does not exist. This is not however, what Sankara argued. Certainly it is possible through the diligent application of yogic principles, to transcend the everyday world, and be united with Brahman. In such a case, one becomes a jivanmukta, or a person who is united with Brahman, while still alive in the everyday world. In such a case the liberated person attaches no significance whatsoever to the empirical world, but lives within Brahman. Nevertheless, even in such a case, the person still has to exist within the empirical world, and to that extent the latter still retains its sense of reality. In summary then, the empirical world still exists with advaita, but its importance diminishes as the individual nears a sense of union with Brahman.

THE BHAGAVAD GITA

The Gita is perhaps the most famous and widely read Hindu scripture. It was originally, part of the much longer epic The Mahabharata. The Bhagavad Gita is a metaphysical and mystical text, yet at the same time a very practical manual providing advice on the way human beings should live their lives (Easwaran, 1975). The spiritual analysis and advice which constitutes the principal part of the Gita is set within the context of a battle scene. The prince Arjuna is drawn up in the ranks of his army, standing in his chariot on the battlefield of Kurukshetra. As he stares across the battlefield at the opposing ranks, he can see individuals who are related to him. He begins to feel the futility of war and wonders whether he should fight. For advice he turns to his charioteer, who is also the God Krishna. Although based on a real historical conflict, the battle scene is probably better considered as a metaphor, whereby the anticipated battle represents the battle of the individual human being to live a moral life within a very imperfect world.

In chapter 2 of the Gita, Krishna starts by advising Arjuna that one should not abstain from acting in the world, or working towards a particular goal, but that one should be very careful not to anticipate any outcome. Yoga consists in not wishing for or expecting any particular result from what one does. In this way we can remain calm and balanced, and finally, through remaining detached from any expectations in life, we can attain union with Brahman. Later, Krishna speaks of two different ways of attaining knowledge of God. One of these ways is through renouncing this world, and giving up material objects. The other method is to work and interact with the world, but at the same time to devote all one's work to the supreme Brahman. Krishna explains that although both methods lead to Brahman, the better method is that of working and devoting one's work to Brahman.

In chapter 6 of the Gita, Krishna describes the characteristics of the yogi. He is described as someone who is in a state of equanimity with his environment, and whose life is characterized by moderation. In later chapters, Krishna emphasizes the importance of thinking continually about God, and of dedicating all one does to God. Indeed there are clear references to a sense of merger with the Divine stressing in effect the mystical nature of the text. Time and again, the Gita stresses the abandonment of desires about the world. In its place, we are advised to cease thinking about what the world might give us, and simply to focus our minds upon Brahman. This devotion to God is central to the bhakti or devotional tradition in Hinduism, a long-standing movement which continues to this day.

THE BHAKTI TRADITION

There have traditionally been many different ways in which devotees within Hinduism have expressed their love of the supreme God. One of the characteristics of Hinduism is that there are a very large number of manifestations of God, and different religious groups focus upon a different aspect of God. Some provide offerings to a statue of God, and may pray and chant His holy name. Meditation upon God is another traditional method of demonstrating devotion. Finally, the focusing upon God during all parts of the day is a popular method of showing devotion. In the sense that everyone, of any social caste or standing could demonstrate devotion to God, the bhakti movement was extremely democratic. It did not rely upon any form of religious hierarchy, and indeed, all members of society could express their love of the Divine. The bhakti movement did therefore represent something of a challenge to religious orthodoxy and to the traditional organization of religion.

The bhakti movement first developed in southern India, and then gradually spread throughout the country. In the medieval period, there was a rapid development of the devotional movement, with the so-called Sant tradition. Ramanuja was a founding figure of this tradition, and overall there was a great emphasis upon the love of God as a mystical pathway, rather than the reading of scripture or the engagement in complex philosophical speculation.

Ramanuja was born in the eleventh century CE, in southern India near to the present-day city of Chennai (formerly known as Madras). He was born into a well-educated Brahmin family and from an early age showed both a strong disposition for the spiritual life, but also for an unconventional approach to caste distinctions. As a young man, for example, he made close friends with another young man, of

a much lower caste. Ramanuja was committed to a devotional interpretation of Hindu scriptures, and was personally committed to the
worship of Brahman. Through his personal approach he came into
conflict with a number of other teachers of the period, and insisted
on remaining true to his own beliefs. Ramanuja consistently argued
against the idea of Indian thought as involving a withdrawal from
the world, and emphasized the significance of the love of God.

Another significant philosopher of the bhakti movement was
Madhvacharya, who was probably born in 1238 CE near the town of
Udipi, in the state of Karnataka. He also placed emphasis on devotion to a personal God. However, perhaps the most celebrated member of this movement was Kabir. He was born right at the end of
the fourteenth century, and raised in a Muslim family near Benares.
His poems and philosophy traverse the boundaries of all religions
and schools of thought in India. He has been held in great esteem
by Muslims, Hindus and Sikhs, and indeed many of his hymns are
included in the Sri Guru Granth Sahib, the holy scripture of the Sikhs.

From a theological point of view, Kabir believed in the importance
of the individual soul and its relationship with the universal soul. For
him, the mystical quest involved working towards the merger of the
two. He was deeply influenced by the teachings of the other members
of the Hindu Sant tradition, but also by Sufi mystics. Kabir was a
strong advocate of the unity of all religions. He did not wish to align
himself with one particular religion, and preferred to think instead
of a simple, loving devotion to God, without conceptualizing God as
belonging to a particular religion. Linked to this perception of the
interrelationships between religions was the distaste held by Kabir
for the external manifestations of religious practice. He did not advocate or like ceremonies which, for example, resulted in a form of religious discrimination whereby those who had wealth and influence
were able to use religion to further their influence.

Approximately a century after the birth of Kabir, another leading
bhakti philosopher was born, whose teachings were to have a considerable impact upon the contemporary world. Chaitanya was born
in 1486 CE in Bengal, and practised devotion to Krishna, besides
studying Sanskrit and the scriptures. In the modern age, perhaps
the most celebrated advocate of the teachings of Chaitanya, has been
A. C. Bhaktivedanta Swami Prabhupada, who established the International Society for Krishna Consciousness (ISKCON).

YOGA

Yoga incorporates a range of methods and approaches ranging from meditation to asceticism, and mantras to physical postures, which are used as techniques to unite the individual with the Divine. Yoga adepts use a combination of methods to achieve their goal, whether physical or psychological. There is some debate about the meaning of the word yoga in terms of its etymology, but it is usually related to the Sanskrit word meaning to unite or to yoke. There is an apparent connection here with the idea of joining the individual soul to the cosmic soul. Nevertheless, the term yoga also possesses the connotation of a spiritual discipline, and a means to achieve a particular goal. In summary then, we can conceive of yoga as implying both the means of achievement, and the actual mystical goal itself.

The path of yoga has traditionally been conceived to consist of not one, but several different routes to a mystical union. Karma yoga is the route involving devout action and works dedicated to the Divine. By acting unselfishly and doing one's duty, the aspirant can make spiritual progress towards union with God. Bhakti yoga is the path of devotion, whereby through prayer, ceremony, or the use of mantra, the aspirant continually dedicates thoughts to God. In Jnana yoga, the devotee concentrates on acquiring knowledge of God, and by this means is able to approach the Divine more closely. There are, in addition, a wide range of practical techniques which are used by the aspirant to reach closer to God. These include the practice of postures and the use of meditational techniques, and are summarized under the title of Kriya yoga. Finally, Raja yoga is the employment of a combination of these techniques to attain mystical understanding and experience. The different approaches to yoga were originally described, albeit in a succinct form, in Patanjali's *Yoga Sutras*, written around the second century BCE.

In the West, yoga has become traditionally known through the use of the kind of techniques practised within Kriya yoga, and especially through the postures of Hatha yoga. The latter is sometimes taught, along with yogic breathing exercises, as a fundamentally physical activity, although many teachers also emphasize the spiritual aspects of Hatha yoga. There has also been an interest in the West in the more esoteric aspects of yoga, such as Tantric yoga, and these approaches have to a varying degree been adopted by 'new age' religions. The use of tantric techniques starts from the assumption that the divine energy present throughout the universe is also present to an extent in all of us, and great spiritual benefits may be obtained if we can acquire means to utilize that energy. Tantric approaches have traditionally been regarded as unconventional, and in India orthodox brahminical belief has tended to reject many of the beliefs and practices of tantra. The affinity between tantric practices and orthodox Vedic belief remains a matter of debate among both scholars and practising Hindus. The first Westerner to describe tantra in a scholarly manner was probably Sir John Woodroffe who died in 1936, and who had been a judge in India, during British colonial rule. He had become interested in the subject, and tried to describe tantra in a systematic and objective way.

One particular aspect of tantra which has attracted interest is that of the kundalini. Within this system of yoga, there is assumed to be a source of energy located at the base of the spine in each individual, which through various techniques can be utilized effectively. This source of energy is sometimes conceived as a divinity or as a serpent. Through the use of meditational or breathing techniques, the individual has the capacity to awaken this source of energy. In doing so, the energy source or kundalini can move up a channel within the spine, and ultimately result for the individual in a form of enlightenment.

The sheer variety of yoga practises may appear confusing, and make it difficult to see anything which unites this diversity into a coherent whole. Nevertheless, there are certain key features and assumptions within all variants of yoga. Fundamentally yoga is concerned with the relationship between the individual spirit or soul, and the external universe. The purpose of yoga is to enable the individual to achieve a sense of harmony between the internal self and the world. In achieving this joining together of the individual and the universal, the person will first of all acquire psychologically a sense of peace and harmony, with a mind which tends not to become anxious or to waver depending upon changes in the external world. At the same time, the individual will tend to react in a balanced and even-minded way to external events, including relationships with other human beings. The practitioner of yoga will aim for an existence which is in total harmony. To put it another way, one might say that the yogi aspires to achieve the fullest and most complete understanding of his or her own humanity.

It could also probably be argued that yoga, while deriving from a Hindu cultural background, does at the same time transcend particular religious traditions. Certainly the postures or asanas of Hatha yoga and the breathing exercises of pranayama can be used as part of a programme of physical health quite separate from any religious belief. As they do not involve any specific spiritual commitment, they could also be incorporated into other patterns of religious practice. It could also be argued that the idea implicit with yoga, of the individual merging with the absolute, is an idea sufficiently general to be capable of adapting to a variety of religious contexts.

SANKARA

As mentioned earlier Sankara was the leading Indian philosopher and mystic, who articulated the doctrine of advaita Vedanta. He was born in the village of Kaladi, in the state of Kerala, probably around 788 CE. There is some uncertainty about the actual year of his birth, and some consider that he was more probably born in the early years of the eighth century CE. The exact date of his birth is perhaps less important than the breadth and authority of his teaching and writing. He was born a Brahmin, but his father died when he was about seven years of age leaving the family relatively poor. Sankara was an only child, and his mother would no doubt have preferred him to enter a secure occupation rather than pursuing the role of a wandering religious mystic and teacher. Yet from an early age it seems that Sankara was inclined towards the spiritual life. His mother arranged for him to undergo the Brahmin initiation of the sacred-thread ceremony, but would not apparently agree to the young Sankara becoming ordained as a wandering monk. Nevertheless Sankara would not abandon his ambition.

Various legends and traditions have been transmitted both orally and in writing concerning the life of Sankara, and it is difficult to establish an absolute authentication of them. However, an often-repeated story suggests that Sankara was one day bathing in a river, when he was attacked and gripped by a crocodile. He thought he was beyond rescue and would certainly be killed. Under these extreme circumstances he decided to take the personal vow of becoming a sannyasin, or wandering holy man. Within Hindu tradition, such a vow taken under the serious threat of impending death is regarded as valid. However, he managed to escape from the crocodile. Sankara subsequently made arrangements for the safety and care of his mother with relatives, and promised her that he would return to officiate at her funeral service. He then departed on the first of what would be many spiritual journeys around India. His first intention was to find a teacher who would become his guru, and complete the sannyasin vow which he had made to himself. He eventually met a Swami Govinda at Badrinath in northern India, who agreed to be his guru and to complete his education. After tuition with Swami Govinda, he set off on another journey during which he wrote his most famous works, his commentaries on the Brahma Sutras, the Upanishads and the Bhagavad Gita. These commentaries have remained classics of Indian philosophy to this day.

For the remainder of his relatively short life, Sankara devoted himself to the life of a wandering ascetic, who taught and engaged leading religious figures in debate. He developed a reputation across India, for his wisdom and knowledge of the scriptures. Sankara founded maths or monasteries in various parts of India, and kept his promise to his mother to officiate at her funeral. He died at Kedarnath in the Himalayas, when he was 32 years of age. He is still regarded as one of the leading spiritual figures and mystics in the history of Hindu thought.

SWAMI VIVEKANANDA

Vivekananda was arguably one of the leading mystics and spiritual teachers of the modern age. In particular, he articulated for a new audience, the teachings of advaita Vedanta. He was born in 1863 in Kolkata, Bengal. His original name was Narendra Nath Datta, and he only acquired the name Swami Vivekananda later in life, a name which reflected his role as a Hindu sannyasin. For convenience, we will refer to him as Vivekananda.

In 1881 Vivekananda, who had had strong spiritual and religious leanings since being a young boy, made the acquaintance of a monk and teacher called Sri Ramakrishna. He became a disciple of Ramakrishna and studied under him for several years. It was also about this time that he enrolled at the University of Calcutta. Sadly, in 1884, the year in which he graduated, his father died. Vivekananda became more and more involved in a small group of disciples of Sri Ramakrishna, although two years later in 1886 Ramakrishna himself died. The community of monks tended to look towards Vivekananda as their spiritual leader, and shortly after Ramakrishna's death, the group of monks formalized themselves into a community dedicated to following and putting into practice the teachings of Ramakrishna.

Several years later, Vivekananda set off on a series of pilgrimages around India, partly to learn from his observations of the diversity of India, but also to try to clarify his feelings about his role in life. He had in childhood been brought up in a relatively affluent family situation, and was now profoundly affected by the poverty which he observed around India. He was determined to try to do something about that poverty, and in that was very much influenced by the teachings of Ramakrishna in relation to the importance of religious people trying to work for the benefit of society. Vivekananda gradually developed a philosophy which combined the traditional spiritual teaching of Hinduism, with the pragmatic, scientific-oriented philosophy of the West. He argued that the best way forward for India was to combine the best aspects of East and West. In particular, he took the Vedanta teaching of the atman, or individual soul, and stressed first of all that it was important for people to recognize the ultimate purity and perfection inherent in the atman, and to work towards this in a spiritual and mystical sense. In addition however, he also stressed the importance for Indian people of learning from the technology of the West, to try to bring about improvements in their material lifestyle. One of the most important results of his reflections was the establishment of the Ramakrishna Mission as an organization dedicated to among others, the achievement of these goals.

In 1893, Vivekananda was invited to attend and speak at the World Parliament of Religions held at Chicago. His speeches there made an enormous impact, and provided the Western audience with insights into Indian mysticism. Vivekananda's fame spread as a result of his lectures, and he was invited to stay in the United States to teach. He met leading academics and also visited England. In 1897, he returned to India, and during a very busy schedule, founded the Ramakrishna Math at Belur. He made one more visit to the United States, but returned to India in 1900 where he died in 1902.

Vivekananda was a Hindu mystic, but his concept of humanity and of religion, transcended that of his own religion. He was a strong advocate of the unity of all faiths, and recognized that all religions were ultimately aiming towards the same goal. He viewed the soul of each individual as being just one element of the universal soul or Brahman. This helped him to conceptualize all human beings as being linked together, and needing to take responsibility for each other's welfare. Besides being a mystic, he also recognized the importance of being pragmatic in life, to improve the quality of life of the poorest people.

KEY IDEAS

Central to Hindu philosophy is the concept of the atman, or individual soul, being united with Brahman, or the universal soul. Through this process, the individual achieves moksha, or release from the cycle of birth and rebirth. Advaita or non-dualism, a philosophy particularly associated with the teachings of Sankara, proposes the idea of the essential lack of differentiation between the individual and Brahman. The philosophy of the Bhagavad Gita is explained, in terms both of the nature of the individual mystic, and also of the approach of bhakti or devotion to God. The different approaches of yoga are discussed, including both the physical asanas of Hatha yoga, and the more spiritual aspects of the philosophy. Finally, the lives of mystics such as Kabir and Vivekananda reveal a number of similarities in terms of lifestyle and belief.

CHAPTER 10

SIKH AND JAIN MYSTICISM

SUMMARY

This chapter examines the mystical elements in two Indian religions, Sikhism and Jainism. Sikhism is discussed in terms of its monotheism and the way in which an individual can aspire to a close relationship with the Divine. There is a summary of the techniques used by Sikhs to achieve a union with God, such as the repetition of the name of God. The key beliefs of Jainism are summarized, including the emphasis placed upon the ascetic lifestyle and the avoidance of harm to other living things. There is a summary of the life of Mahavira.

THE SIKH TRADITION

Sikhism is perhaps not generally thought of as a mystical religion, and yet the idea of a union with God is at the heart of the religion. Sikhism arose and developed during a period of considerable religious conflict, and this arguably makes it an even greater achievement that the Sikh gurus were able to create a coherent corpus of religious belief and practice, and also an established route by which the individual could form a direct relationship with God.

Sikhism is very much a monotheistic religion. Perhaps the clearest statement in the Sikh scriptures of the nature of God is provided by the so-called Mul Mantra. This was probably written by Guru Nanak, the first Sikh guru, and was later placed at the very beginning of the Sikh scripture, the Guru Granth Sahib, when this was compiled some time later. The key principles espoused by the Mul Mantra are that there is one God, who is present in all things and who sustains all of life and existence. God has no form or shape and hence cannot really be conceptualized. God was present at creation and is not affected in any way by the passage of time. In fact, God is beyond such a concept as time, and is unaffected by the cycle of birth and death associated with living things. Individuals may strive very hard to know and understand God, but in the final analysis God decides through his grace, to whom he will pass an understanding of himself, and to whom he will reveal himself.

Sikhism developed in an environment deeply influenced by Hinduism and by Islam. Unlike Hinduism however, there is no sense at all within the Sikh religion that God can become incarnate. God is ultimately not capable of being known in his entirety. Although the universe is continually changing and evolving, God is beyond such processes, and is the one stable element in the universe.

However, for the individual to attain a mystical understanding of God, it is first necessary according to Guru Nanak, to purify the mind. Guru Nanak starts his analysis with the assumption that the human being has a tendency to live in a condition of maya or delusion. In other words, human beings tend to be preoccupied with the material world. They seek to acquire possessions which they believe will provide them with a comfortable life and do not focus sufficiently upon the needs of others. They do not give sufficient attention to the moral dimension of life seeking continually for those possessions or activities which they believe will bring them happiness. When they are thinking in this way, people are exhibiting a characteristic termed haumai. This term means approximately that the individual is focusing too much on the ego and the self. The individual is continually thinking about his own needs and not those of other people. The term haumai encompasses notions of selfishness and acquisitiveness, but it is really more than that. It suggests a preoccupation with the self and the ego, on every level. The person who is living with such a philosophical approach to life is termed 'manmukh' or someone who focuses continually on the 'man'. The vowel in this word is pronounced approximately like the vowel sound in 'fun'. The term 'man' designates something similar to the mind of a human being. A person who is manmukh concentrates all the time on his own mind and his own aspirations for life. He thinks less about others, and does not focus sufficiently upon God and spiritual matters. The ultimate purpose of the Sikh religion is to encourage the individual to be much less manmukh, and to be much more focused upon God and a religious way of life. When this is achieved, the individual is described as gurmukh, rather than manmukh. The individual is now focused upon the Guru, or God (Shackle and Singh, 2005).

The person who is gurmukh is devoted to the spiritual life. He or she typically dedicates actions to God, rather than pursuing activities in a selfish way. In the person who is gurmukh, there is an all-encompassing dedication to the spiritual life. The person's goal is to dedicate his life in all its aspects to God, to practice his religion diligently, and ultimately to seek such an understanding of God, that in a mystical sense, he can merge his own existence with God. In Sikh theology, a central importance is given to the concept of the nam or name of God. It is by focusing upon the nam that a person can attain a profound understanding of God and ultimately a sense of union with the Divine. An understanding of the nam leads to a person becoming gurmukh. However, the nam is not simply an appellation for God, but a means of conceptualizing God, and a focus for meditation. The concept of nam symbolizes the spiritual truth which is part of God. When a person focuses upon the nam, he or she is concentrating upon all the noble values inherent in God, the understanding of the true spiritual way which is inherent in God, and upon God's role in creating and sustaining a universe which has an implicit moral structure.

The name of God is perhaps the central element in the methods which are used by Sikhs to reach the ultimate state of a union with God. The first method is that of nam japan, which means the repetition of the name of God. This is in someways a similar method to the use of mantra in other religions. The individual repeats or chants the name of God over and over again. The Sikh scriptures do emphasize however, that this should not be simply a routine repetition, but that during the process of nam japan, the individual should give careful thought to God and to the purpose of the process.

The other method associated with nam japan is nam simaran, which is a process of meditation and reflection upon the name of God and everything which is signified by that. The word 'simaran' means something like 'remembering' in the sense of bringing continually into one's mind. It thus carries implications of making a serious effort to reflect upon the name and qualities of God. This remembering might take the form of meditating upon several verses from the scriptures, and thinking carefully about their meaning. However, it might involve the thoughtful participation in prayer or the singing of hymns.

Although it is almost certain that a general participation in the life of the Sikh community, with its customs and practices, is a significant help in reaching salvation, nevertheless, the practices of nam japan and nam simaran are the key methods used in developing a closer and closer relationship with God, through a series of stages. The final stage is that of sahaj or a condition of mystical union with God. The person who attains this stage of spiritual development moves beyond the process of birth and death, and there are perhaps parallels with the concept of moksha or release, within Hinduism. The attainment of sahaj only happens, however, through the granting of God's grace. Certainly individuals must make their own efforts to achieve sahaj, but God must also intervene in the process. In addition, the attainment of sahaj results in the elimination of haumai, and the individual living a life of being focused upon God and upon the welfare of others. A person living in this way is living in accordance with the will of God. This is often termed the hukam. This word signifies the sum total of God's concept of existence in terms of leading a moral life, helping others, thinking about God, reading and reflecting upon the scripture, the Guru Granth Sahib, and leading a life in harmony with the principles laid down by Guru Nanak. Such a person can be described as gurmukh.

THE CONTEXT OF SIKH MYSTICISM

The ultimate purpose of the Sikh tradition is to obtain liberation from the cycle of birth and death, and to achieve a sense of union with God. However, the Sikh mystical tradition does in no sense suggest a withdrawal from the world to achieve this goal. To some extent this is a point of difference between Sikhism and the Hindu context in which it developed.

The Sikh tradition stresses that the life of the Sikh should involve the normal activities of family life. In this sense, the mystical goal is not something which is separate from the normal, everyday business of living, working and raising a family. Religion and daily life are seen as being inextricably connected. Moreover, the spiritual life informs and assists the conduct of the individual in daily life. Although of course, this same approach applies also to many Hindus, there is also within Hinduism the tradition of the ascetic withdrawing from society to pursue a life of meditation and contemplation. This tradition tends to be absent within Sikhism.

Linked to this belief in the importance of the connection between the spiritual and the practical business of daily life is the idea of making a contribution to the lives of others. It is seen as very important to make a contribution to society in general, and in particular to the lives of the needy. If one were to concentrate only on one's own salvation, then that would not be seen as ultimately very ethical. It would need to be combined with a care for others. This idea of service to society is reflected in a variety of ways. Sikhs will give of their skills and expertise to help others, and also to try to alleviate any human suffering, whether among the Sikh community, or within the wider society.

One particular example of service which is very much associated with Sikh society is the langar or community meal. When Sikhs come to the gurdwara or Sikh temple for a religious service, a free community meal is usually provided. This is normally paid for by voluntary contributions, and all the preparation and serving is done by volunteers as an act of service. There are also other features of the langar, which reflect wider aspects of the ethics of Sikhism.

In the time of Guru Nanak, there were many quite rigid conventions about the serving of food within the Hindu tradition. The nature of one's caste tended to determine with whom one was permitted to eat. Guru Nanak considered such customs as fundamentally divisive within society, and the custom of the langar was at least partly to encourage all people, of whatever social status, to meet and eat together. There was thus a strong sense of social ethics attached to the concept of the langar from the beginning. In addition, the food served at the langar is normally vegetarian, partly to make the food acceptable to anyone, of whatever religious tradition.

The sense of social equality which is a part of the langar tradition is found within other areas of Sikh life. There is, for example, no separate role of that of priest within Sikhism. Any individual may, in principle, lead the prayers at the gurdwara. Most gurdwaras, however, do have someone who both looks after the building, and conducts important ceremonies. This role is that of the granthi, and the individual may be paid a small allowance. It is not however a role comparable to that of an ordained priest in another religion.

THE GURU GRANTH SAHIB

The Sikh scripture is called the Guru Granth Sahib or the Adi Granth. The scripture holds a very important place in the faith, and is in fact considered as the 'spiritual teacher' or Guru of Sikhs. It is perhaps, at least partly for this reason, that there does not exist a priesthood, for the Guru Granth Sahib itself provides the authoritative teachings of the faith (Singh, 2005).

Guru Nanak was the founder of the Sikh religion, and after him there were another nine gurus who were both the spiritual and secular leaders of the Sikh community. The final guru was Guru Gobind Singh, who in 1708 decided that after him, there would be no more gurus, but that the Sikh scripture would be the Guru. The precise reasons for this decision are unclear, but one can at least reflect upon the consequences. From a religious perspective, one of the major effects was that there was from then on, clear and precise spiritual guidance which would be less affected by interpretation. To some extent this also contributed to a more egalitarian community, since there was no religious hierarchy.

An interesting feature of the Guru Granth Sahib is that it contains many examples of writings by religious figures who were not Sikhs. Such writers include Ramanand and Ravidas, Sheikh Farid and Kabir (Vaudeville, 1998). Their inclusion demonstrates a respect for other faiths. To this day, the Sikh community combines a profound pride in their own religion, with a sense of religious tolerance and respect for other faiths.

The main work of compiling the Adi Granth was carried out by the fifth Sikh guru, Arjan Dev. He decided to do this, because there already existed numerous writings by the previous Gurus, along with the writings of the so-called bhagats or religious figures who were in sympathy with the Sikh values and approach to religion. There was a danger that, unless this increasingly voluminous text was harmonized and systematized, there would develop many different variations of the scriptures. Guru Arjan enlisted the help of Bhai Gurdas, and the two of them began work on ordering and structuring the material in 1599 CE. It was a complicated task involving the integration of the work of the first five Gurus, including that of Guru Nanak, fifteen bhagats, and a number of other contributors. The Adi Granth was finished in 1604, and placed in the Golden Temple at Amritsar. Guru Gobind Singh, the last human Guru, added further text, and then finally declared in 1708 that this version would be regarded as the Guru of the Sikh community. This has been accepted since that date, with the content of the Guru Granth Sahib being regarded as inspired by God, and also as a source of guidance for the lives of all Sikhs.

Since the content of the Guru Granth Sahib is regarded as divinely inspired, there are very strict prohibitions concerning even the slightest alteration of the text. The scripture is written in the Gurmukhi script, which is regarded by Sikhs as itself having some religious significance. This is to the extent that it is considered important for Sikhs to be able to read the Guru Granth Sahib in the original language. To try to control the publication of unauthorized versions of the Guru Granth Sahib, there is only one authorized publisher of the scripture, and this is located in Amritsar in the Panjab. So sensitive is the act of publishing this text, that if any imperfect copies are produced by accident during the printing, then these are destroyed in a form of religious ceremony.

In keeping with the high status of the Guru Granth Sahib, it is treated with a great degree of respect and reverence at the Sikh temple or gurdwara. In the large prayer hall of the gurdwara, the scripture is placed on a platform at one end, and the granthi of the gurdwara sits behind ceremonially fanning the holy book. When entering the prayer hall, Sikhs should cover their heads and remove their shoes, as a mark of respect to the Guru. They should also bow to the Guru before sitting down. As the entire congregation sits on the floor of the prayer hall, the Guru Granth Sahib is always at a higher level than that of the people present. This symbolism is also often observed in a Sikh home, where a copy of the scripture will usually be kept on a high shelf, for example, at a higher level than the height of an average person. In the evening at the gurdwara, when the day's religious activities have been completed, the Guru Granth Sahib is 'put to bed' in a ceremony in which a special prayer is said. The holy book is covered carefully with clean material, until the next morning's religious activities resume.

The Guru Granth Sahib is an important element in many of the ceremonies which are part of the Sikh family life. When a baby is being given a name, the Guru Granth Sahib is opened at random. The first verse on the left-hand page is then read, and the first letter of the first word indicates the first letter of the new name. A name is thus selected having that first initial letter.

As has been mentioned previously, the Guru Granth Sahib is particularly noteworthy because of the eclectic nature of the authors who are included. Kabir is one of the most famous bhagats, and he was born right at the end of the fourteenth century. He was a particularly interesting spiritual figure because he avoided belonging to any particular religious denomination or tradition. This enabled him to be able to contribute to most religious traditions. Kabir belonged to the informal Sant movement which was present in northern India at this time. The Sants were very much opposed to the formal hierarchies of the established religious traditions, and hence were great supporters of social equality. In addition, they practised forms of devotional activity, which gave them some commonalities with the Sikhs.

Kabir was very much opposed to the idea of existing within one particular religious ideology. He probably felt that this was too restrictive, and denied the full extent of the unity between the principal religions. He thus regarded himself as neither a Hindu nor a Muslim, but was at the same time devoted to some aspects of both faiths. In particular, he believed firmly in the idea of a single God, who was the same in all religions. Much in common with classical Hinduism, he perceived the individual as having a soul, which through leading the life of a mystic, could be united with the universal soul of God. This tolerance of other faiths was a fundamental element of the world-view of Guru Nanak.

In conclusion, it is worth noting one of the key terms of Sikhism which, however, occurs only rarely in the Guru Granth Sahib. This is the term waheguru. It refers to God, and points to the entire aim of Sikhism, that is, the mystical union between the individual and God. Used as an element in one form of Sikh greeting, waheguru is also used as a mantram during meditation. Waheguru is the ultimate reality to which Sikhs aspire. Let us now consider some of the key features of the life of Guru Nanak, the founder of Sikhism, examining his life very much from the perspective of that of a mystic.

GURU NANAK

Guru Nanak was born in Talwandi, in the Panjab area of northern India in 1469 CE. As a young boy he showed a strong predilection for the study of religion, and it is recorded that at least one of his teachers felt he was so able and intelligent that he had little left to teach him. This may be an apocryphal story, but it seems likely that his parents found him rather difficult to manage. At about 9 years of age, he went through the sacred-thread ceremony, although he appears to have used the situation to make one or two negative comments about the nature of such ceremonies.

Nanak was married at the age of 16, but did not demonstrate a great interest in establishing himself in a career. Things do not seem to have improved very much from his parents' point of view during his twenties, when despite remonstrations from family members, he did not seem to commit himself to a job. His interests seemed to be developing in the direction of religion and mystical engagement. The birth of two sons in his late twenties did not seem to alter anything. Eventually Nanak agreed to move to Sultanpur and to live with his elder sister and her husband. Here he was given a fairly responsible administrative job in the area. Nevertheless, his interests remained primarily in the area of religious practice. It is recorded that one morning he went to bathe as normal in a local river, but never returned. Local people assumed he had drowned, but he reappeared after about three days. He appears to have had some kind of mystical experience during this period.

It seems that this point represents the complete transition in Nanak's life from trying to meet his responsibilities as a family man, to becoming in effect a wandering mystic and teacher. He set out with his friend Mardana, and travelled eastwards in India, along the Ganges valley, stopping at towns along the way to preach and to hold discussions with local religious leaders. They then turned southwards, before turning back north towards the Panjab. Guru Nanak's next long journey was to travel to Mecca, during the course of which journey he held many discussions with Muslims. The broad theme of his teachings was that people should not become obsessed with the external features and customs of religion, but should try always to concentrate upon the nature of God.

After a number of journeys and pilgrimages, Guru Nanak settled at Kartarpur. Here he founded a religious community, composed of people who had been influenced by his teachings. The community was self-supporting, growing their own food, and working at small-scale craft occupations. Guru Nanak travelled between neighbouring villages while he lived at Kartarpur, but tended to devote himself to religious and meditational activities. Finally, Nanak died at Kartarpur in 1539. He left a large body of teachings, and was characterized in his lifetime, by comments frequently made about the need to be tolerant of different religions, and in particular to ensure tolerance between Hindus and Muslims.

THE JAIN TRADITION

Like the Sikh tradition, Jainism as a religion was started and developed within a Hindu context. The two faiths evolved in different directions, but they at least share a common beginning. Moreover, Guru Nanak would have come across groups of Jains in the Panjab area of India. The two faiths would thus have some familiarity with each other, even if they did not mix a great deal. There are however, some significant differences, most notably perhaps the differences in terms of lifestyle. As has been argued, Sikhs are very much devoted to the idea of conventional family life, whereas for the Jain community there is at least the ideal of the ascetic, far removed from the warmth of family and society. However, the one aspect which links them firmly together is a strong element of mysticism in their overall spiritual life.

Jains follow the teachings and traditions of enlightened beings called tirthankaras or 'ford-builders'. These enlightened individuals are people who have managed through spiritual discipline to eliminate the adverse effects of accumulated karma, and hence to spiritually cleanse themselves. The metaphor contained in their name is that they have crossed over the river to a state of purity and enlightenment on the other side. More than that perhaps, they are now able because of this enlightenment to assist others in the spiritual quest for enlightenment, and to help them also in 'crossing the river'. Jains consider that there have been 24 tirthankaras within recorded history, and that the latest, and perhaps most well known, was Mahavira, who was born in approximately 599 BCE and who died in approximately 527 BCE.

Central to Jain belief and ethics is the notion that all living things, from human beings to the smallest organism, have a soul. This central belief has fundamental consequences for the entire Jain worldview. The souls of all living things are viewed as equal, and hence Jains are extremely careful in their actions towards the natural world. This affects everything from the food which they are prepared to consume to the type of work which they will undergo. They consider that each individual soul possesses certain pure and noble qualities to which it is the responsibility of each individual to aspire. The sum total of these profoundly good qualities is the main element of the Jain concept of God. In other words, God is not conceived as a supreme, all-powerful authority, but rather as the sum total of the virtues present in the individual soul.

One of the consequences of this view of the soul is a profound sense of compassion towards other living creatures. Jains would always take the greatest care not to harm another living creature. For this reason, Jains are completely vegetarian in their diet. There is an element in the Jain world-view, which involves a sense of renouncing the world. Jains view the world as to some extent very unsatisfactory, and it is only by leading an extremely pure life that one can move beyond this impure earth, and escape from the cycle of birth and death to liberation (Roy, 1984).

The principles of vegetarianism are reflected in a number of ways in the life of Jains. They will certainly avoid eating meat, fish and eggs, and will be extremely careful in trying to ensure that no small insects or animals are accidentally killed during the preparation of food. Jains have traditionally always filtered their drinking water, to avoid consuming small creatures. Wherever possible they will also pass water back through the filter in the opposite direction to ensure that any small creatures are able to return to their original environment. Although Jains will inevitably consume plants as part of their diet, they will always try to reduce the damage to plants to the minimum. They will be especially careful, for example, in withdrawing plants from the soil, since this act may kill or damage small animals living in conjunction with the plants. It is for this reason, that Jains often avoid the consumption of such plants as potatoes.

Jain monks and nuns tend to be very ascetic in their lifestyle, in keeping with their view of the unsatisfactory nature of the world. Lay people within Jainism will follow these practices to some extent, and will, for example, try to take up an occupation which does not involve any sense of violence or aggression to another human being, whether directly or indirectly. Jain monks and nuns are well known for the practice of sweeping the path in front of them gently with a light brush, to try to move aside any small living thing, to avoid treading upon it. Jains will also wear a kind of mask over their mouths when reading from scriptures or when they are near holy statues, in a temple, for example. This is to avoid the possibility of droplets of saliva landing on the holy books or images.

As the everyday world is viewed as unsatisfactory, Jains try to avoid becoming attached to the world, including to possessions and to the pleasures of life. This is one of the key elements in the path to attaining liberation of the soul. By avoiding becoming attached to the world, the Jain can develop good karma, which will help in the goal of attaining moksha or release from the cycle of transmigration. Fasting is a particular feature of this view of renouncing the world. There are a variety of different fasts practised by Jains. Sometimes a Jain will fast as a reminder that he has not maintained sufficiently high standards in his life. In particular, a well known and perhaps contentious Jain practice involves fasting to death. This is sometimes done when a person has reached an advanced age and realizes that the main part of life is now over. When the person has reached a stage of feeling tranquil about life, and feeling a sense of equanimity, the person may decide to embark on a final fast to death. The person will refuse food, and perhaps water too. It is regarded as a very devout spiritual exercise. However, it is perhaps understandable that in contemporary India, some people have raised concerns about the practice of apparently deliberately taking one's own life. Jains, however, do not quite view it in that way. They see it rather as the final spiritual discipline of a life devoted to strict religious principles.

It is perhaps worth noting that Mahatma Gandhi was greatly influenced by Jainism. As a child he was aware of Jain principles, and all his life held very dearly ideas such as non-violence, the importance of fasting, and a strong empathy for other human beings.

Jains have a philosophical view of the world which could be described as relativist. They do not consider that any single perception of an issue can be expected to indicate absolute truth. Rather, there exist in the world many different interpretations of reality, and according to Jains one should try to appreciate and respect these to understand the world. One of the results of this philosophical view is that Jains exhibit a great deal of tolerance towards other religions.

One of the principal mystical techniques used by Jains is that of meditation. The main purpose is for the individual to be able to identify with the noble, constant qualities of the individual soul. As human beings we tend to become preoccupied with the evolving nature of the world, and this type of meditation tries to help the individual to return to the noble, eternal qualities within. Let us finally look at Mahavira in terms of what we know about him, and his reflection of the nature of mysticism within the Jain religion.

MAHAVIRA

Mahavira, or the 'great hero' was the Indian mystic who brought together the key ideas and beliefs of Jainism into a coherent religious and philosophical system. Many of these ideas had existed before developed by the preceding Tirthankaras. The latter were enlightened mystics who spent their lives trying to help other Jains achieve enlightenment. Jains believe that there were 23 such beings before Mahavira, and that Mahavira was the 24th and final tirthankara. Mahavira took the ideas which had evolved over the centuries, and disseminated them throughout India gaining in the process, many followers.

Mahavira is thought to have been born in 599 BCE in what is now the state of Bihar. His parents belonged to the nobility, and hence Mahavira was born into a life of relative comfort and affluence. However, early in his life he showed a tendency towards the religious life, and as a young man he relinquished his family wealth and status leaving home to become a wandering mendicant. He led the life of an ascetic travelling widely throughout India to pass on the teachings of the Jains. His essential teaching was that all human beings accumulate the consequences of their actions as karma, and need to live an extremely ethical life involving also meditation, to eliminate the effects of their karma, and obtain release from the cycle of endless births and deaths. Mahavira is thought to have died in approximately 527 BCE.

KEY IDEAS

Although Sikhism and Jainism are very different faiths, there are some points of similarity. They both place considerable emphasis upon personal restraint in various ways. In terms of eating, Sikhs are not as exclusively vegetarian as Jains, although certainly in the case of food served at the gurdwara, Sikhs are vegetarian. There is a strong mystical trend in both religions. In Sikhism, liberation is achieved through meditation and the intervention of God, whereas in Jainism there is not the same concept of God, and liberation is achieved much more through personal discipline and meditation.

PART III

THE PURPOSE OF MYSTICISM

CHAPTER 11

THE MYSTICAL GOAL

SUMMARY

All mystical thought and practice is directed towards a higher spiritual goal, a sense of closeness to God within the terms of theistic religions, or a sense of unification with some spiritual force in the case of other belief systems. This chapter explores the nature of this ultimate goal. It examines the different terms used to describe this final state, whether that be liberation, union or enlightenment, or a different term. Although this subject is by its nature difficult to describe, the chapter tries to understand something of the intensity and significance of the experience for the individual seeker.

INTRODUCTION

Mystics are indeed spiritual seekers. They are not satisfied with the rewards of a life dedicated to the physical world. For them, the world of work, the home or the family, while offering many rewards, is insufficient to complete their purpose on this earth. They need something else, and that other purpose is a sense of closeness with the spiritual force which had a role in their personal creation, and to which they hope to return upon their physical death. For the true mystic this search for a return to this spiritual entity is an overwhelming desire, something which they find impossible to deny. For many, the search means relinquishing the everyday world, and assuming a life of solitude and reflection.

The goal to which they aspire is conceptualized differently in different religions, and it is an interesting point of reflection and analysis, whether all mystical goals are ultimately the same experience.

It could be argued, for example, that all mystics are fundamentally aspiring to the same end, but that different aspects of this goal are emphasized in different religious traditions. However, one might argue that to be aspiring to the same goal in very diverse religious traditions seems rather improbable, and that there are basic differences between the different traditions.

ENLIGHTENMENT

We can analyse this problem further, by considering the types of terms employed to describe the goals of mystical seekers. The concepts used do not of course reveal everything about the end state, but they do provide an indication of that to which the seeker is aspiring. Within Buddhism, for example, there is the general aim of enlightenment. The goal of enlightenment is based upon the notion of replicating the original experience of the historical Buddha. It suggests first and foremost a new vision of the world, a new way of looking out at the nature of existence, and the nature of human relationships. The enlightenment experience is often described by Buddhists in terms of language which suggests that one is able to see and understand the true reality of the world, or to see the material world as it really exists. Different metaphors are sometimes used to illustrate this enhanced vision. There is a sense in which the enlightened person can see clearly for the first time, and it may be compared to looking through a window pane which was dirty, but is now sparkling clean.

In contemporary language, rather than that of the historical Buddha, we might conceptualize enlightenment as a psychological state, rather than any relationship with an external entity. In other words, it is entirely within ourselves, and self-dependent, rather than having reference to externals. There is also a sense of the capacity of human beings who are enlightened to return to some former state in their lives before they became affected by, or conditioned by, the complexities of the modern world. This is often likened to seeing the world again with the vision we had as a child. We view the world with a kind of innocence which we gradually lose as we get older.

One aspect of enlightenment which often attracts criticism is that it can appear to be an egocentric goal. In other words, people may undergo long periods of meditation or mystical training to achieve a psychological state which makes them feel happier about themselves or which fulfils them in some way. However, some might ask whether this psychological state benefits anyone else in any way. A Buddhist would probably argue that being in an enlightened state enables one to relate much more effectively to one's fellow human beings, and to be a better-functioning human being.

Much the same might be argued for the Hindu concept of liberation from the cycle of rebirth. The liberated person is freed from concerns for the material world, and may live a life withdrawn from the daily concerns which preoccupy the majority of human beings. Again, someone might raise the ethical question of whether such a goal is fundamentally moral. It could be interpreted as withdrawing from the arguable responsibility of all human beings to work towards a better life for all. The pursuit of union with God could be seen as coming within the same category. While it is true that those regarded as very spiritual and in close communion with God may be seen as role models and as a source of inspiration for others, some may view the pursuit of such an apparently abstract purpose as uniting with God as too vague to be of general utility. However, such concerns do not appear to have dissuaded mystics in the past, and probably will not turn others in the future, from their spiritual path.

THE IDEA OF A UNIVERSAL SPIRIT

In some religious traditions, the ultimate goal of the mystic is almost beyond linguistic analysis, and almost impossible to conceptualize. In the Taoist tradition, there is the conception of the universe being guided by an all-pervading principle, the Tao. The mystical goal is to reunite oneself with that cosmic principle, and hence return to the source of energy from which one came. However, this principle is both external to us and inside us, at the same time. In other words, it is not a question of uniting ourselves with something 'out there'. It is more a case of realizing who we truly are ourselves, of recognizing that by our very nature we are united through the Tao, with everything else in the universe.

Within the Tao philosophy the person who has developed to the highest spiritual level is able to act fully within the principle of wu wei. This is the philosophy of acting in a completely relaxed and natural manner, but taking such action as seems entirely appropriate in the circumstances. We are often socialized into the idea that we must struggle, strive and work extremely hard to achieve our goals in life. To some extent this is true, but the Taoist points to a slightly different

perspective on this. The principle of wu wei suggests that the spiritually adept will be able to recognize those aspects of a situation when
it is more appropriate to relax and to take no action, and those times
when effort is necessary. The Taoist adept is therefore able to live
much more in tune with life and their surroundings. The philosophy
is not one of abandoning our responsibilities and living a rather
trivial existence. Rather it is a question of being wise, and trying to
identify situations when intervention and action would be appropriate, and when it would probably be more sensible to leave a situation
alone.

The Taoist mystic views the world from the perspective that it is
adequate for itself. This means that if the world is left to resolve its
own imbalances then it will generally succeed in doing so, without
the intervention of human beings. We can envisage this on an environmental level, where the world has, over the millennia, reached a
dynamic equilibrium. If there are natural imbalances, the ecosystem
can adapt itself reasonably well. A natural forest fire, for example,
will temporarily destroy the vegetation, but during the next growth
season seeds germinate and shoots appear, and it does not take too
long for the forest to regenerate itself. Unfortunately, the intervention
of human beings can result in large-scale and more long-lasting
damage. The Taoist mystic understands the equilibrium of the world
and tries always to act in such a way that the equilibrium is maintained as far as possible.

Now in terms of the personal characteristics of someone this
may sound rather vague. In someways it may be true that it would be
difficult to recognize a Taoist mystic immediately from their actions.
They may seem much like anyone else at first meeting. However, after
knowing them for some time, we might begin to appreciate that they
reacted rather differently to certain circumstances. Perhaps certain
events might not irritate them quite as much as we might expect with
another person; perhaps they might be a little more reflective when
taking a decision; and perhaps they might seem a little calmer in
some situations than we might expect. If we had the opportunity to
live alongside them for some considerable time, then we might begin
to notice a general difference in approach to life, compared to many
other people. In other words, recognizing the qualities, the personality, and the approach to life of Taoist mystics is not something which
can be achieved in a brief meeting. It requires a relatively long period
of sustained contact to understand their world-view.

Much the same is true of other mystics. It is generally true of all spiritual traditions that the aspirant is required to live and work for a long time in the company of their teacher or guru. This period may last for many years, and during this time the aspirant may do many simple jobs around the monastery, or may serve the guru by preparing food or doing other chores. The formal religious training may be a relatively minor element in the whole process. However, the purpose of this lengthy apprenticeship is for the aspirant to live alongside the teacher in ordinary, everyday circumstances, and to gradually appreciate experientially the guru's philosophy of life. The aspirant learns slowly how to react in certain circumstances, and how to relate to others. This is not taught intellectually, but by example. This method is seen par excellence, in the traditional approach to spiritual training in India, where a young boy may express a wish to attach himself to a guru for a long period of training.

Mystical training is an activity where experiential knowledge is generally more important than intellectual knowledge. We may understand a truth such as the interrelationship of the elements of the natural world, on an intellectual plane, but behaving in accord with that principle may be a different matter. We may not know how best to live our lives according to that principle. In individual situations we may not know how best to react. It is here where sustained contact with a spiritual teacher is of help.

The Tao is a matter of recognizing our true nature, and our true relationship with everything in the world. When we have achieved that we have not, in a sense, become anything very special, we have just become ourselves. True, we have perhaps become ourselves in our most human form, but externally people may not see anything very different in us.

Much the same is true of enlightenment or satori in the Zen tradition. It is often repeated in the literature on Zen, that if we were to become enlightened then there is nothing special to say about it, except perhaps that we see the world clearly, whereas previously we did not. Indeed to talk about Zen, or to discuss it, is almost a contradiction in terms because Zen is really beyond conceptual analysis (Watts, 2000). It is a way of looking at life which is completely natural, and which does not really require the application of reason and logic. However, even though Zen is ultimately experiential in nature, we still try to reach for words to articulate that experience. Like Tao, however, the Zen experience is, in the final analysis, the capacity to simply live our lives in a natural, fulfilled way. This is Zen mysticism!

Mencius, the Chinese sage who followed in the tradition of Confucius, appears to have had a spiritual philosophy not dissimilar from Taoism and Zen. For him, ultimate enlightenment involved at least partially, stilling the mind, and being able to place oneself in communion with the divine energy of the universe. For Plotinus, the Egyptian philosopher and mystic born in 205 CE, the mystical quest involved a gradual and determined elimination of the external trappings which hindered the progress of the soul towards the ultimate. In his view, the human soul was encumbered by associations with the material world, and when these were shed, there could be a gradual progress towards union with the Divine.

THE CONCEPT OF NON-ATTACHMENT

Most mystical traditions appear to agree on the importance of eliminating a concern for the material world. Mystics generally emphasize the importance of devoting themselves to their spiritual life, and not to a preoccupation with everyday matters. To varying extents they try to eat only simple food, they do not wear ostentatious clothes, they live in simple accommodation, and often will not involve themselves in financial transactions of any kind. One of the consequences of this type of lifestyle is that it appears to free them to some extent from concerns and anxieties about life. They appear less concerned about decisions they have taken in the past, or things they might have done or not have done, and they also are less anxious about the future. Unlike most people, mystics appear to be able to reduce their preoccupation with future events and what might happen. The result is that they are able to live much more in present time. Part of the consequence of this is that mystics appear able to live life much more intensely. If they are talking to someone, for example, they are able to focus entirely upon that conversation, rather than their minds wondering about where they are going next, or what they will be doing later in the day. For most of us, our minds are so continually active, moving rapidly from one perceived problem to another, that we rarely have the capacity to concentrate on the present moment. Mystics appear to be able to achieve this, and it also seems to be a largely general characteristic throughout different religious traditions.

It seems to be generally true of mystics that they are not overly concerned with future events. In a well-known statement of this position, Jesus advised people in the Sermon on the Mount to 'take therefore no thought for the morrow: for the morrow shall take thought for the things of itself' (Mt. 6.34). Most traditions of mystical training appear to incorporate a range of activities designed to encourage the aspirant towards 'letting go' of the world, or to be 'non-attached'. No doubt some human beings are, by virtue of their natural disposition, more able to do this than others. However, it probably remains one of the most difficult things for people to achieve. We spend most of our lives gradually becoming more and more attached to things, and indeed it may be that we are genetically inclined to become attached to people and objects. If we were not 'attached' to our children, then we would be much less inclined to want to protect them and help them grow to adulthood. Equally, we would not be as inclined to provide a stable home for them. In other words, we would probably be more dysfunctional as parents. However, that very attachment to the world, its people and its objects can lead us to a distorted view of life. We can become obsessed with caring for and protecting ourselves and others. Mystics are able to keep these obsessions in balance. 'Letting go' of the world is not a question of ceasing to care about what happens, or of adopting an attitude of complete indifference. This would be unethical, and would in a sense be the opposite of having a sense of humanity towards the world. However, the approach of the mystic is to care for others and for the world, while at the same time not become preoccupied and obsessed with events. Peter Matthiessen records that on departing for a long journey into the Himalayas, the advice from his Buddhist teacher consisted of two words 'Expect nothing' (1979: 272). This advice points to the same principle. When we are contemplating a new venture or a journey, we tend very easily to develop expectations and hopes for what we will achieve and experience. And yet such expectations can destroy our ability to understand and gain something from the present. We find ourselves always living in the future, and continually waiting for our anticipated goals to come to fruition. The Buddhist teacher was pointing to this phenomenon, and indicating that the most appropriate way was to have no expectations. Life would then just unfold naturally, and we would be able to experience it in all its variety, without any preconceptions.

In Sufism, the ultimate goal of mystics is to eliminate all concerns for the individual self. This state is termed fana. It is not, however, simply a condition of not being attached to worldly possessions, but also includes the idea of not anticipating anything to be received from the world. Within a Sufi world-view, however, the state of fana is not a question of ceasing to exist, but rather of existing, not for the self, but for God. The Sufi mystic acts and exists entirely for God, a condition known as baqa.

THE NATURAL WAY

One aspect of the mystic approach to life is that the mystic is apparently able to act in a completely spontaneous manner. Mystics appear to have the capacity to act and behave in a natural manner, relating to other people and taking decisions in such a way that they do not become overly concerned with what might be considered the 'correct' or 'acceptable' decision. They are not overly preoccupied with the opinions which other people have of them. They do not feel the need to impress others, and to act in accord with preconceived notions of the way things ought to be done. They are confident within themselves that they will find naturally the best response to a situation. They are not conditioned in this by expectations of others, and in particular by religious orthodoxy or teachings. Inevitably this sometimes leads mystics into conflict with those around them. They may simply be viewed as too unorthodox or subjective for other people, who may reject their apparently individualistic world-view.

LOVE AND DEVOTION

Jewish mystics have always emphasized the importance of love towards one's fellow human beings. Importantly, this sense of love should not be demonstrated simply towards those who we like, but also towards those with whom we do not feel an affinity. In other words, it should be an unconditional sense of love. Mystics generally demonstrate this approach to their fellow human beings. This profound sense of love leads mystics towards a position in which they do not make judgements about people. While mystics may, on the one hand, have a very clear concept of right and wrong, they do not withhold their love from those who do not act ethically. They are thus not necessarily moral relativists, in the sense that they may feel that there are innumerable moral positions to take on a question, which are all acceptable. While holding that one moral position may be more acceptable than another, at the same time they do not pass personal judgement, and do not condemn another for taking a different moral stance. This type of approach has from time to time led mystics to spend time in the company of social outcasts, demonstrating their idea of universal love by helping others. Just as mystics cultivate a profound sense of love for God, they also transmit this love for others.

This emphasis on love within Jewish mysticism has a great deal in common with the concept of nirvana within Buddhism. Within Mahayana Buddhism the concept of the bodhisattvas who dedicate themselves to the spiritual well-being of others on the pathway to enlightenment places the focus upon the ideal of showing love towards others. Some people may form the view of mystics within all traditions, that they are essentially pursuing their own form of truth, principally for their own sake. There is, however, little purpose in gaining what we might term enlightenment, if the purpose is for the glorification of the individual. Ultimately, it would be a contradiction in terms to describe oneself as enlightened, yet working solely for one's own benefit. Most mystics follow a similar principle to that of the bodhisattva, which is to use one's own enlightenment and wisdom to assist others.

This is particularly true of the bhakti tradition within Hinduism. Bhakti mysticism focuses principally upon achieving a state of loving devotion towards God. This is viewed as the primary mystical goal. However, as all human beings are perceived as containing an element of God, devotion to God is also considered as a profound sense of care for all people. This view of life has led bhakti mystics to devote themselves to the care of the sick and the dispossessed, and to view such charitable works as being an essential part of what it means to be a mystic devoted to the Divine.

Once the devotees of the bhakti tradition develop a profound sense of love for God and for all of humanity, they are lead to have, in varying degrees, a sense of universalism in religion. They tended to encourage their followers to avoid the minutiae of religious observance, and to concentrate on the basic principles of the faith. In some cases, such as that of the celebrated Indian mystic Kabir, there was an advocacy of the essential unity between religions, including particularly Islam and Hinduism. Kabir was probably born in 1398 CE in Benaras (Varanasi). According to popular tradition he was born a Hindu, but was adopted while young by a Muslim couple and raised as a Muslim. Although trained by his new family in their occupation as a weaver, Kabir showed tendencies towards the spiritual life, and managed to persuade Ramananda, a famous Hindu mystic, to take him as a student. Ramananda belonged to what is termed the Sant tradition of northern India. The Sants were a diverse group of wandering mystics, who believed essentially in the aim of achieving a union with God, while attaching little or no importance to many of the conventions of Hindu and Islamic orthodoxy. They rejected, for example, the orthodox practices of the Hindu caste system. They were almost certainly regarded as too unconventional by the religious hierarchies. In a sense he advocated the unity of God, whether the God of Hindus or of Muslims. He was equally influenced by Sufism as by Hindu mystical traditions. Perhaps in accord with his rejection of religious hierarchies, he always tended to communicate in his verses in the language of ordinary people of the time, rather than in a literary style. In someways Kabir demonstrates many of the archetypal characteristics of the mystic. He is devoted to God, and concentrates on a sense of union with God to the exclusion of all else. This single-minded devotion leads him to view many of the ceremonies and conventions of organized religion as being superfluous. Equally his love for other human beings, and in particular the poorer members of society, appears to motivate him to suggest that they ought not to become caught within the detailed observance of religious rites. One might see a form of religious socialism here. He does not wish to see ordinary people caught within the undue influence of the religiously powerful. Such was his appeal at the time, that he was an influence upon the Sikh religion and many of his verses were included in the Guru Granth Sahib. His poetry still retains considerable popularity in contemporary India.

PEACE AND EQUILIBRIUM

One of the characteristics which one tends to associate with mystics is a sense of peace and equanimity towards the world. They tend to have a balanced outlook on life, and do not respond in an extreme fashion to circumstances, however testing. In some cases, such an outlook on life may arise through a profound confidence in God and the care which he demonstrates for humanity, or it may arise from the form of mystical training undertaken. In some mystics this particular perspective on life may develop from having an understanding of the nature of equilibrium and harmony in life. This is demonstrated in traditional Chinese philosophy, and in particular within Taoism, by the concepts of yin and yang. These two concepts are usually illustrated by a so-called Taijitu image, which shows two swirling, interrelated areas, one black and one white. The black area represents the yin, while the white area represents the yang. This conceptualization points to the nature of the opposites in the world, which are in a state of dynamic equilibrium. Such a state of equilibrium is perceived to exist in both the natural world and in the internal, psychological world of the human being. Examples of opposites in the physical world include heat and cold, and light and dark. It is an often-cited truism that we would find it difficult to appreciate cold, unless we had experienced heat. Our understanding of the world is based at least partly, upon our appreciation of the opposites which exist. However, the natural world adjusts to these opposites. Plants have developed strategies to cope with temperature differences at different times of the year.

Just as nature has found mechanisms to maintain a form of equilibrium, human beings are adapted by both their physiology and psychology to maintain a form of equilibrium. The various biochemical feedback mechanisms and control systems ensure that if one element of the body's physiology alters, other processes can often manage to adapt so that the overall condition of the body does not change. In other words, the body reacts to restore the natural equilibrium. Similarly, in the case of psychological difficulties the body is able to adapt. We are able to learn strategies to cope with problems, and not necessarily to overreact to them. We learn throughout life, that sometimes if we can manage to live with a difficult situation, and to give the circumstances time to change, that this is exactly what happens. Even seemingly very difficult situations will often gradually improve, given time. When we look back on an event which seemed extremely difficult at the time, it is often quite amazing that it has gradually improved, sometimes without any specific intervention. Of course, this does not always happen, but there are many occasions on which it does. In other words, as human beings, our lives and our relationships with other human beings are also in a type of dynamic equilibrium.

When things go wrong, as they must do from time to time, they may gradually return to some form of equilibrium. This is the nature of existence to which the Chinese philosophy of yin and yang points. Mystics of all religious traditions, often appear to understand the nature of equilibrium in existence, and be able to behave and react to events with a sense of balance. They do not overreact when things go wrong, nor do they especially become excited when things go well. They appreciate that these are just elements of the overall balance of the universe, and that it is unwise to react too quickly to changing events. Eventually a move in one direction will be corrected by a move in the other. Thus mystics often demonstrate a wise understanding of society, and the way in which it develops.

Meditation often points to this ebb and flow of ideas and of feelings. When we are meditating we notice that ideas sometimes flow into the mind. They may remain there and cause us some anxiety, as we try very hard to make them go away. Sometimes however, if we relax and let such ideas fade away, they may gradually disappear from consciousness. The rise and fall of ideas in the mind tend to parallel the situation in the external world.

It is worth noting however that when one is meditating within either the Tao or Zen traditions, it is not the purpose of meditation to try to achieve something or some state, in particular. In fact, the attempt to achieve a particular mental state is really the antithesis of Zen or Taoist training. Within the latter one simply meditates without the goal of trying to achieve something. In fact, the attempt to achieve a goal would be rather dysfunctional in the overall terms of meditation (Watts: 1975).

In many different mystical traditions, one finds the principle that mystics do not try to be always achieving something. In Western culture there is the sense that one should always be trying to achieve more, to expand one's life, to acquire more possessions or to gain more successes. The person who is happy with the way things are, is sometimes regarded as being much too passive. Passivity is not viewed in a positive way. One is expected to continually strive after a larger house or a better job. It is not seen as desirable to reflect simply on the way things are at the present time, and to be contented with this situation. The mystic, however, values the quality of the way things are in the present moment. The mystic has truly recognized that expansionism is not a recipe for happiness, and that to be always striving for something else is not conducive to peace and contentment.

DUALISM

A way of expressing this rather technically is to speak of dualism, and the dualistic nature of life. In a contemporary, capitalistic society we do tend to live in a dualistic way. This means that while we think of ourselves and our own identities in this life, we then think of the rest of the world and of existence as being separate from us. We see a separateness between our own identity and the rest of the world, including those things which we would like to acquire, or to achieve or to become. We do not view ourselves as being a part of the same world, but as separate from the world. This dualism tends to result in a psychological approach to life whereby we wish to gain something from this separate part of the world. We do not see the essential unity of things, but the separateness of existence.

Mystics, however, tend to view, or try to view, the world as a unity. They see themselves as part of the rest of the universe. This sense of unity relates not only to the physical environment, but also to other people. This non-dualism then also creates a particular approach to ethics, since if we are actually part of everything else then we would not wish to harm it. On the contrary we would want to sustain it, and to support it (Maezumi, 2001).

In human existence, dualism becomes apparent in very subtle ways. For example, human beings seem to have an almost unlimited capacity for thought. While thinking is clearly an essential activity, it is important to appreciate that thought is not the same as the object of thought. When we think about something we are employing concepts to stand in the place of the things which we are thinking about. We play about with those concepts, manipulate them in our minds, and dream up all sorts of possibilities with those concepts. However, when we do this, we are living in a very unreal world. The manipulation of concepts is really a kind of fiction. The mystic appreciates that the thinking process is an artificial means of understanding the world, and does not really result in true understanding. To achieve a genuine understanding of the world, one must concentrate on the events themselves.

As human beings we tend to be reflecting continually on events in the past, and worrying whether we did the right thing. We also tend to be thinking about the future, and whether we will be able to cope with events which arise. The overall result is that we become very anxious because we find it difficult to cope with the uncertainty of the world. The events around us are continually changing, and we find it equally difficult to cope with this continuous change, whether in family life or in the workplace. The mystic, however, tries to resolve these dilemmas by attempting to live in the present moment with great intensity, so that each and every aspect of life is fully appreciated and understood. This attempt to live in the present, rather than being preoccupied with the past and the future, appears to be an almost universal characteristic of the mystic consciousness.

KEY IDEAS

Many terms are used to describe the goal of mystics. The sheer multitude of terms used probably reflects the complexity of the concept which they seek to describe. The idea of describing such a subjective and interior experience as the goal of mysticism is almost impossible in words. It is for this reason that this area of religion is so often described using imagery and metaphor. However, some relatively precise terms do persist in use. Enlightenment describes the mental state of a person, who, after a course of spiritual training, has a clearer and more precise view of the world than one might expect in an untrained individual. It is particularly used to describe someone who, in the Buddhist tradition, attains a state comparable to that achieved by the historical Buddha. Hindus frequently speak of liberation, in the sense that the soul is released from the endless cycle of transmigration. The soul is free and can merge with the eternal. Many mystical traditions have a concept of 'letting go' or of non-attachment to the world. This reflects the idea that spiritual progress cannot be achieved while the individual is still attached to the material world. Once the individual can set aside concerns associated with the physical world, then progress can be achieved. Finally, there is the abolition of a sense of dualism; or alternatively, one might speak of the attainment of a state of non-dualism. In other words, in the latter case, the individual achieves a sense of unity or union with the Divine, in a condition in which there is no sense of separation between God and the individual.

CHAPTER 12

MYSTICAL AND ORTHODOX TRADITIONS

SUMMARY

This chapter examines the contrast, and sometimes conflict, between mysticism and traditional religion. It explores the contrasting views that there may on the one hand be simply one general form of mystical experience, or whether mysticism on the other hand is an experience unique to each faith. The chapter also examines a range of new religious movements and their associated mystical beliefs and practices.

INTRODUCTION

Most of the main faiths of the world are more than simply a set of religious beliefs. At their heart of course is a spiritual world-view, but they are all to varying degrees interrelated with legal and political systems, and also in some cases, wield considerable economic power. Though this may be true nowadays, so much more was it true in past ages.

In medieval times, and even today to some extent, if the religious basis of a faith was challenged even to a slight extent, there was an implicit or indeed actual challenge to the other dimensions of the faith, including the political dimension. Very few leaders are happy to yield political power to others, and hence the doctrinal basis of a faith was usually defended to the ultimate extent possible.

Mystical traditions have always been very subjective in approach, and indeed challenging to the more established, orthodox aspects of a religion. They may even at times have challenged the core teaching of a faith. The result has been that mystics have often been regarded as rather dangerous, and certainly a threat to the established faith.

This has not always resulted in persecution, but nevertheless this has sometimes been the outcome. Mystics have sometimes tried to exclude themselves from society, reducing the possibility that they would cause antagonism with the local political leaders. On other occasions, they may have joined together in religious communities, which although existing largely within society, nevertheless maintained a certain degree of separate existence.

In some cases it may not be clearly evident that one can contrast mystical belief with the so-called orthodox traditions within a faith (Baldick, 2000). First, it may be that a religion is sufficiently diffuse in its key principles that it is not very clear what would count as a contravention of the main teachings. Secondly, it may be that a religion does not possess a central authority which takes decisions concerning alleged deviations from the main teachings.

There have traditionally been two main perspectives on the nature of mysticism (Clarke, 2000). First, mystical experience is largely the same across a range of different faiths. Thus, although the terminology may be different, and even to some extent there may be differences in practice, the fundamental experience, it is argued, is largely the same. On this view, mysticism almost becomes a form of religion itself, albeit without the scriptures, doctrine and ritual normally associated with a structured religion.

Secondly, it can be argued that mysticism, or indeed a particular school of mysticism, is inevitably a product of a specific religion and of the accompanying culture. Within such a perspective, the mystical belief system is connected with the particular religious culture within which it has evolved. It might be argued that within the latter model there is much more likelihood that a mystical system may be seen juxtaposed with the more orthodox tradition of the faith. It is here that there is arguably more room for tension between belief systems, and what, in the middle ages, was termed heresy.

RELIGIOUS TOLERANCE

Paradoxically, it can sometimes be that a religion which is very tolerant of other faiths actually generates considerable conflict with other religions. This is arguably true of the Baha'i Faith. One of the central assumptions of the religion is that human beings undergo a form of spiritual evolution (Gouvion and Jouvion, 1993: 16). In other words, there is the assertion that when religions have arisen in the history of humanity, they have tended to do so because the particular historical and social context was ready for that particular belief system. Each faith contributed to the particular stage of development of human beings at the time, and was then ultimately superseded by further religious insights at a later date. This view perceives humanity as undergoing a long process of spiritual development, and indeed continuing to do so. Each religion adds something unique to the development of human spirituality. According to Baha'is, there will be further spiritual insights to come, which will add yet more to our awareness of the world of faith.

On one level this may seem a reasonable assertion, in that it proposes a distinct contribution from each religion, while at the same time not setting one belief system against another. However, for many members of individual religions, there is the implicit or explicit belief that their own religion is a closer representation of the truth than other faiths. *A fortiori*, they may also believe that their own religion does represent a certain finality in terms of a statement about humanity and the Divine. In other words, they may believe that there is nothing to add to their religion, and that all has been said. It is difficult to rationalize a world-view which sees the human race as being on a spiritual journey, with a view which considers that a particular religion has to all intents and purposes made the final statement on human religious life.

The Baha'i Faith also presents a rather different, relativistic picture of God (Momen, 1997). Baha'u'llah, the nineteenth-century Iranian mystic who founded the Baha'i Faith, argued that ultimately there was only one God. However, members of different religions and different cultures could only possibly visualize specific aspects of that God. It is important to realize, argue the Baha'is that the culture within which we are brought up, affects our capacity to understand and conceptualize God. Fundamentally, however, the limitations of human beings prevent them from seeing and understanding all facets of God. This explains why within different faiths there exist different concepts of God.

Clearly such a philosophy can be difficult for adherents of some religions to accept. Followers of a monotheistic religion, for example, may find it problematic to consider God as they perceive Him, to be equivalent to the Tao of Taoism. If unity as a concept is central to the idea of mysticism, then Baha'is do represent a definite mystical trend in religion. Not only do they perceive the many different notions of God as being manifestations of the Divine, but further they contend that basically all religions point to the same sense of truth. Such beliefs, while being harmonious in their world-view, may result in conflict with those who have a strong sense of the individuality and validity of their own belief system. Indeed, since the establishment of the religion, members of the Baha'i Faith have been subject to extensive and violent persecution in different parts of the world. Despite this they have sustained a number of principles which are at the heart of their faith. These include an extrapolation of the principle of theological unity to a sense of global unity, and a firm commitment to the essential unity of all human beings. The latter belief has led Baha'is to a comprehensive social policy, designed to help all those who are disadvantaged or who are suffering in someway. They have also, in keeping with this philosophy, maintained a deep commitment to gender equality.

NEW RELIGIOUS MOVEMENTS

The Baha'i Faith is a relatively recent religion, although there are many more religious groups which have evolved or are evolving in contemporary times. Such 'new religious movements' very often encapsulate a strong mystical trend. They are often, although not always, characterized by the presence of a charismatic leader, who may determine to a large extent, the spiritual direction of the group. In smaller groups, such a leader may exercise direct and even autocratic control over the group members, whereas when groups grow larger, very often an administrative structure or hierarchy develops which is not dissimilar from that found in an orthodox religion.

Some new religious movements are radically different from established religions in terms of their world-view or theology, whereas others appear to represent reasonably orthodox views, even though they have many of the other characteristics of new movements. Traditions such as Hinduism, which are themselves very varied in terms of practice, ritual and customs, have been the inspiration of many new religious movements. The tradition of the guru within Hinduism has perhaps also encouraged the development of new groupings. It does not seem at all strange, for example, within Hinduism for a teacher to gather around himself or herself a group of devotees, and to in effect start, if not a new religion, at least a new spiritual tradition. This has happened frequently throughout the history of Hinduism, and the practice continues in contemporary times. What is perhaps different in modern society is the presence of mass and electronic communications, which enables new groups to communicate their ideas rapidly, and hence gain worldwide interest. The connection between such religious movements and popular culture, particularly music, has also facilitated this process.

One Hindu-oriented movement, which grew from very small beginnings in New York, to become a global movement, was the International Society for Krishna Consciousness, or ISKCON. This movement was established by a university-educated Bengali mystic, A. C. Bhaktivedanta Prabhupada. Although maintaining a lifelong interest in Hindu mysticism, Prabhupada lead an orthodox life of working and bringing up a family. In his late sixties, however, he decided to develop his lifelong devotion to Krishna, into a new movement, by seeking new devotees in the United States.

The movement itself was founded upon what could be regarded as orthodox Hinduism. It traced its teachings back to the sixteenth-century mystic Chaitanya, who did much to encourage the bhakti movement in India, and to encourage the worship of Krishna. For this movement, salvation was to be found in a devotion to Krishna, and the dedication of all one's actions to God. The ultimate mystical aim was through devotion, to be able to obtain release or moksha from the cycle of rebirth, so that one could gain a mystical union with God. Devotees of the movement were characterized by the practice of chanting the so-called Hare Krishna mantra, and dancing to the accompaniment of drums and cymbals. There was nothing particularly unorthodox about this in terms of Hindu tradition, although it did seem culturally different on British and American streets when first encountered in the 1960s.

There was thus no real schism between such a 'new' movement and orthodox Hinduism since there was no significant difference between the teachings. Nevertheless, the clash with traditional religion came perhaps not from the teachings and theology, but from the social practices of the movement, particularly in terms of raising money to finance the organization. When Prabhupada started the group in 1965, a good deal of money was raised through either donations, or through the sale of books published by the organization. However, as this gradually proved inadequate to finance a rapidly growing organization, the movement diversified into selling a range of products to the youth culture of the 1970s. Although retaining its original

Hindu teachings, the organization does not now have the same profile in the public consciousness. The death of Prabhupada in 1977 had an adverse effect on the growth of the movement. One can see here a pattern which is repeated with some other new religious movements, where the membership of a movement finds it difficult to sustain the movement in the absence of the original leader.

In the case of the Rajneesh movement, a noticeable decline took place during the life of the founder, although the movement has continued in a less-ostentatious form. The movement was founded by Chandra Mohan Jain, who was born in 1931 in India. He was known for the majority of his adult life as Bhagwan Shree Rajneesh, although later in life he took the name Osho. He was well educated, and well versed in Western and Hindu philosophic traditions. While a university lecturer, he travelled extensively in India, giving lectures on spirituality, self-development and mysticism. It was during this period that he acquired a reputation as a rather unconventional teacher, particularly with regard to his advocacy of sexual experiences outside normal social conventions. He established an ashram at Poona, and later in 1981 moved to the United States to found an ashram in Oregon. He attracted a great many Western devotees, who became 'sannyasins' in the movement. His organization became extremely wealthy, and one of the external criticisms made of Rajneesh was that he did not adopt the personal asceticism characteristic of many spiritual leaders and mystics. There seems little doubt that Rajneesh was an impressive teacher, with great charisma, who exercised extensive influence over the members of the organization.

Rajneesh was a leading figure of what could be termed the spiritual counterculture movement of the 1960s and 1970s. In his teaching he drew widely from a range of religious traditions, both Eastern and Western. His broad spiritual origins lay in the Hindu advaita movement, although in his teachings one can identify strands which are not dissimilar from the teachings of many well-known mystics. He spoke of the existence of 'truth' as being interior to human beings, rather than residing in compliance with external norms or beliefs. Central to his approach was a very unconventional style of teaching, whereby he would challenge accepted values. This is not unknown in some mystic traditions, and one might see a parallel with the techniques used by Zen masters. Indeed the use of the koan as a teaching technique is designed to break down the approach of rational thought, and to help the disciple to behave more spontaneously and in keeping with their natural self. Rajneesh stressed that life should be lived in the present, a philosophy which recurs many times in the teachings of mystics. This approach may of course be interpreted in a number of different ways, ranging from a meditative awareness of present existence to an apparent justification for an unconventional lifestyle which takes no account of consequences. Rajneesh also emphasized mindfulness, or full awareness of the reality which surrounds one. This is a teaching which one finds in different schools of Buddhism. He also suggested to disciples that they do not try to be continually seeking something outside themselves or elsewhere in life. They should, however, develop the capacity to see reality all around them, and to value the existence which they were able to experience.

Rajneesh emphasized that all human beings could become enlightened and only needed to adopt the correct approach. He developed a wide variety of different techniques of meditation, perhaps the best known being the so-called Dynamic Meditation technique. This involves alternate periods of jumping, spontaneous laughter and singing, dancing, and rapid breathing. He was also famous for incorporating humour within his mystical teaching, and using jokes as a form of teaching. Philosophically, he claimed to be producing a synthesis of Western rationalism, and Indian mysticism. One might argue that although the teachings of Rajneesh was extremely varied, drew upon many traditions, and were at times unconventional, they were not sufficiently different to have caused extensive conflict with religious orthodoxies. If required, Rajneesh could possibly have pointed out parallels between his philosophy and mysticism, and the doctrines of established religion. Ultimately it was perhaps the social organization of his ashrams which caused conflict and indeed outrage in the media. Particularly this was so with regard to the sexual permissiveness within the community, and with the extravagant amassing of wealth which appeared to be endorsed by Rajneesh himself.

A Hindu teacher who appears to have generated relatively little controversy was Maharishi Mahesh Yogi. He was born in 1917, and was perhaps most famous because of his association with the 'flower-power' counterculture of the late 1960s and, above all, his association with the Beatles and other pop singers. He also became well known because of his establishment of the technique known as Transcendental Meditation, which became very popular around the world in the 1960s and 1970s.

After a university education, the Maharishi followed a fairly conventional path for an Indian mystic, in that he had his own guru, and eventually left to establish himself as an individual teacher. In 1957 he founded the so-called Spiritual Regeneration Movement, and a year later started to publicize Transcendental Meditation. The latter was based, according to the Maharishi, on the meditation teachings of his own guru. In 1958 he also embarked on a world tour to spread his teachings. During his life, he would make a number of such tours. He wrote a number of books on meditation and Hindu mysticism, notable being perhaps his translation and discussion of the Bhagavad Gita. In 1973 he founded the Maharishi International University in California.

His real fame came about in 1967 when he met the Beatles, who became very interested in his spiritual teachings, and stayed with him for a time in India. During this period, there was an enormous media interest in the Maharishi, particularly as he associated with film stars and pop singers. Given these circumstances, it is perhaps surprising that very little adverse publicity surrounded the Maharishi. He seems to have managed to maintain his reputation as a serious and influential teacher. This is perhaps partly because his teaching could be perceived as within the mainstream of Hinduism, resting as it did upon such traditional texts as the Bhagavad Gita, but also because the communities associated with him seem to have largely avoided the adverse publicity associated with some other groups.

Although the 1960s and 1970s were to some extent the period of expansion of minority religions and new religious movements, there was also an increasing opposition movement to such organizations, affected to a large extent by allegations of exploitation of young people by 'cults'. Adverse publicity came from a variety of sources, but the many media stories tended to focus upon allegations of sexual misconduct and exploitation, financial exploitation, psychological effects of living within a cult environment, indoctrination and submission of the will to a charismatic, influential figure. The very nature of closed, religious movements makes it very difficult to verify claims. Those within them may not be able to communicate effectively with the outside world because of the rule-making nature of such organizations. This may lead to accusations of secrecy and control over members. However, members who become disenchanted and leave organizations, may be felt to be less than objective when they later make criticisms of the group. Many new religious movements are subject at one time or another to at least some accusations of inappropriate conduct, and the effects of the anti-cult movement has probably had the effect of causing religious organizations to address concerns whether fully justified or not.

New religious movements have developed across the full range of religions. Several have developed with a Buddhist orientation, and indeed have grown into large organizations, with a distinct organizational structure. The Friends of the Western Buddhist Order (FWBO) was founded by Sangharakshita in 1967. It was designed as a Buddhist organization which in terms of teaching, practice and organization was relevant to a Western spiritual context. Although often referred to as a new religious movement, its teachings are very close to what one would find in an orthodox Theravada monastery. The central practice is breathing meditation, where individuals concentrate their attention on the process of inhalation and exhalation. The individual focuses attention on the tip of the nostrils and imagines the invisible breath entering the nostrils during inhalation, and then leaving the nostrils during exhalation. It is an established method for stilling the mind. Inevitably thoughts arise in the mind during this meditation, but the central idea is to keep returning the attention to the inhalation and exhalation. Eventually, the mind becomes much calmer. The other main practice is that of loving kindness. Here the individual focuses the mind upon the idea of being kind to others. In addition, there is the parallel practice of generating kindness towards oneself. One can very easily be too critical of oneself, and not take full cognizance of the pressures one is under when making certain decisions. The practice of loving kindness takes this into account for oneself as well as for other people. In short it is the practice of developing empathy towards others, and of encouraging feelings of kindness towards other people.

In addition the FWBO teaches the concepts of impermanence and of no-self. The notion of impermanence stresses that the world is continually changing, and that hence becoming attached to any aspect of the material world is ultimately futile. It is a central element of Buddhist teaching, along with the concept of no-self. The latter stresses that it is very difficult to conceive of any element within the human being, which constitutes a permanent self. Hence, the idea of no-self encourages the individual to be less egoistic, and more concerned with kindness and empathy towards others. The organization does not raise money exclusively through the conventional

Theravada practice of accepting alms, but through a number of businesses. The FWBO does not have ordained monks and nuns living in accordance with Theravada tradition, but nevertheless it is possible to be ordained. In many ways, the organization adheres to the basic principles of orthodox Buddhism, but has nevertheless found itself the subject of criticism by some members of the orthodoxy, on two main grounds. The first form of criticism is in a sense, religious, in that the founder of the FWBO, Sangharakshita is said not to have originally undergone an orthodox ordination, with the consequence that some argue he is not part of an accepted Buddhist lineage. The idea of the latter is that a teacher should be able, in theory, to trace back the basis of his or her acquired teaching, through a historical line of other teachers, ultimately to the historical Buddha himself. The second criticism is that some have argued that the organization manifests some of the less desirable characteristics of cults, particularly in relation to the alleged exploitation and psychological mistreatment of young ordinands.

It thus appears evident that the teaching and spiritual experiences of the Friends of the Western Buddhist Order are not substantially different from those within traditional Buddhist groups. One is perhaps justified in the assumption that there is no reason why the enlightenment experience should be any different. However, as with other minority traditions it appears that lifestyle and organizational issues are at the heart of any differences or conflict with traditional groups.

This is also certainly true of another new religious movement, the Nation of Islam. This organization has been prominent in the articulation of the rights of black people in the United States, during many of the key historic phases and events of the past century. Still in existence today, it does not now have the high profile which it did in the mid-twentieth century. It was founded in Detroit in 1930 by Wallace Fard Muhammad, who was succeeded in the leadership by Elijah Muhammad. The latter died in 1975. The present leader is Louis Farrakhan, who took over the leadership in 1978.

The Nation of Islam was one of the most important organizations which argued for the complete equality of black people during the important historical period between the 1950s and the 1970s, when after many years of oppression, black people in the United States made a serious claim for equality and dignity in society. The Nation of Islam was active during the same period as the Civil Rights

Movement of Martin Luther King, but approached the issue of equality from a different perspective. While the Civil Rights Movement tended to adopt the non-violent principles associated with Gandhi, the Nation of Islam took a much more assertive approach, claiming and indeed, demanding equality. On some occasions the movement has argued for an independent state for black Americans. In addition, it has done a great deal of social and community work, to try to raise both the economic status of black communities, but also their confidence and pride in themselves.

From a theological viewpoint the connection between the Nation of Islam and with orthodox Islam has always been rather tenuous. One fundamental point of difference, and indeed antagonism with mainstream Islam, has always been the assertion that Allah was incarnate within the body of Wallace Fard Muhammad. The proposition that Allah could appear in effect, within the person of a human being, is completely contrary to the beliefs of Islam. Indeed, it is in such serious opposition to Islam that it is regarded as heretical. For orthodox Muslims therefore, it is impossible to think of the Nation of Islam as a true Islamic organization.

It is interesting that two of the most famous ever members of the Nation of Islam, Malcolm X and Cassius Clay (Muhammad Ali) both became orthodox Sunni Muslims. Malcolm X was born with the surname Little, in 1925, but was always ashamed and annoyed by his inherited surname, as he regarded it as a name derived from former slave masters. He was apparently very able intellectually at school, but as an adolescent the family house was burned down, almost certainly by white racists, and his father died in circumstances which could quite possibly have been a related murder. With a large family to bring up, it appears to have been too much for his mother to bear, and she seems to have had a nervous breakdown. The children were divided between relatives and foster parents. Malcolm became involved in crime and eventually was sentenced to prison. While in prison he met a member of the Nation of Islam, and embarked on a process of self-education. When he was released in 1952, he worked for the organization becoming arguably its leading figure, at a time when the Nation of Islam became very prominent. However, by 1964 there were many political tensions within the organization, notably between Malcolm X and Elijah Muhammad. Malcolm X claimed that Elijah Muhammad was guilty of sexual impropriety with a number of young women working for the organization. The situation became untenable, and Malcolm X left the Nation of Islam. He ultimately made the Hajj pilgrimage to Mecca, and became a Sunni Muslim. It was during this period of his life that he became a leading international figure, and inspiration for many of the developing countries in the world. However, in 1965 the many threats to his life materialized, and he was shot dead in New York while preaching.

The Nation of Islam, from an external perspective, appears to be both an organization for political action, and also a spiritual organization. There seems little doubt that members gain a great deal spiritually from it, and indeed have experiences which can genuinely be described as mystical.

It seems likely that mankind has always had a predisposition towards mystical experience. In ancient times, human existence would have been far more precarious than it is even now. Human beings lived but a short life, clinging to their existence in the face of many dangers, and unpredictable events. Given the capacity to reflect upon their circumstances, they would, perhaps quite naturally have sought some solace in the concept of a powerful external entity, or of some sense of control in the universe. Further than that, having viewed their origins in such a power, they would have had a sense of wishing to unite with it, of, in a manner of speaking, returning home. This is all conjecture of course, for we have little oral or documentary record of times before the existence of the now major world religions. Part of the reason for this of course, perhaps less desirable element of religions, is that they have tried to discourage, or even worse, eliminate, competing belief systems. The very fact that a religion has become 'successful' in terms of adherents, sometimes means that in the past it has tried to varying degrees to reduce the importance of other faiths. Mystical traditions have often, as we have seen, suffered because of this historical pattern.

It seems a reasonable proposition, then, that much of the religious experience of early human beings was mystical in nature. The word 'pagan' has been used for many years to describe religious experience which was outside and beyond that of Judaism and Christianity. The very use of the word reflects the kind of historical trend alluded to above. The word derives from the Latin for someone who lives in the countryside, as opposed to the city. It thus carried connotations in Roman times for people who were rather uncultured and unsophisticated, in comparison with the educated, more sophisticated urban inhabitants. Moreover, it also had the implications of people who believed in the traditional religions and Gods. As Christianity became well established in Roman society, it was very much a religion of the cities. The believers in the new religion were disdainful of the older spiritual beliefs, and indeed, more than that, sought to suppress them. These older beliefs probably involved a strong element of nature worship, of living in close connection with nature and the environment, and of seeing a sense of unity in the world. In other words, there was probably what we would term today, a strong mystical element in their beliefs.

The suppression of the religious beliefs of people, usually minorities, or of people who were less powerful politically or economically, has been one of the less desirable aspects of human history. Often associated with violent suppression and cruelty, it has had the result that many extremely interesting visions of the world, let alone belief systems which were very important to the lives of ordinary people, have been lost to human cultural history. There have been attempts in recent years to revive such belief systems, and hence to create neo-pagan traditions. The clear difficulty however has been the lack of original source material and oral traditions, by which one could trace back traditions, and hence have some form of continuity. Practices and rituals, in effect, had to be invented, and started anew. There are of course, some ideas and traditions of which we still have evidence, for example, in ancient European materials from old Norse cultures, but the task is not easy. There is, however, a growing interest in such attempts to re-create ancient religious traditions, as witnessed by the development of so-called New Age religion.

The concept and term New Age religion developed well over a century ago, although it only started to develop a widespread following with the rise of the alternative spiritualities movement of the 1960s and 1970s. It is extremely eclectic in nature, with a strong mystical element. Among its varied beliefs is the idea that there are spiritual forces in the universe, which have a distinct impact upon human lives, and which can be employed for the benefit of human beings. The nature of these forces is not fully understood, and yet their impact is not generally disputed. This points to the rather intuitive nature of New Age philosophy. This world-view is also holistic in nature, both in relation to the individual human being and to the world and universe. Hence, New Age philosophy and spirituality tend to embrace holistic, natural medical remedies; spiritual healing; ecological methods in agriculture; and the consumption of organic foods.

New Age mysticism draws widely from different religious traditions, but particularly from Eastern religions. It is thus very influenced by forms of meditation, breath control and yoga. The very eclectic nature of New Age has sometimes lead to its being criticized for lack of coherence, and the borrowing at random from whichever tradition seemed attractive for its current purposes. Compared with many religions and traditions it has been more oriented towards feminism than many faiths, and has embraced different aspects of feminist spirituality. Its very eclecticism has also tended to result in approaches which were generally non-doctrinal. It has tended to eschew scriptural approaches, perhaps because it has never attached itself sufficiently strongly to a single tradition or its writings.

In terms of spirituality and mystical approaches, it is difficult to generalize with such a diverse tradition, but arguably the most common approach could be described as pantheistic. There is a general assumption that there is a spiritual force in existence in the universe and that this force is within us all, and we are within this force. The purpose of New Age mysticism, and this is again a generalization, is to spiritually develop the individual to such an extent that he or she is able to unite in a spiritual sense, with this universal force.

Central to New Age philosophy is a pantheistic approach to the world. Of all different philosophies of religion which can claim some element of mysticism, pantheism is arguably, the most representative of mystical thought. It incorporates many of the elements, under one broad heading, which we can identify in a range of major world traditions. It is then perhaps appropriate to end this book with an analysis of pantheistic thought, and of how this manifests itself in contemporary pantheistic practice.

Pantheism is in a sense, theistic, although different pantheists may opt to define God in rather different ways. There is within pantheism, certainly a concept of an external, universal deity or spiritual force, which exerts a generalized controlling mechanism over the universe. It is probably better, however, to conceive of this sense of control as a power which assists the various dimensions of the universe in working together in harmony, rather than as a formal authority. However, more than that, God is also seen as being within all individual parts of the universe – every stick, stone, river, plant and animal. So God is part of everything, and everything and everyone is part of God. We are thus, as human beings, also part of that ultimate power which helps the universe to function effectively. This is very much a mystical idea which is reminiscent of the Upanishads in Hinduism, and also of Taoism. One of the consequences of this is of course a sense of responsibility which we must all bear for the effective functioning of the natural world. Within pantheism, the natural world is of great importance. Human beings are certainly part of nature, but in addition, as creatures with a capacity for technology, it is essential that we remember our linkage with nature, and use that technology wisely, so that we do not damage the natural world. This strong sense of a link with nature is another key mystical idea, and one which is present in a number of religions, for example, Shinto. As part of this sense of respect for nature, there is thus the concept of the way in which all living things are interlinked. A consequence of this idea is a strong feeling that one must be respectful and kind to all people. There is a strong sense of non-violence, and a sense of wishing to help others, partly of course because we are all perceived as part of the same overarching spiritual power.

Furthermore if God is already within all of us, the possession of that divine element signifies that we do not really have need of anyone to intercede on our behalf with God. Hence there is really no need for the role whereby someone acts as an intermediary with God, saying prayers, or interpreting the scriptures. Individuals can perform these functions perfectly well if necessary. Hence the idea of a priesthood becomes redundant, and certainly the concept of a church with its hierarchy is scarcely necessary when each individual person can communicate with God directly. Indeed, God is part of each individual person. Scriptural texts too become to some extent unnecessary in a situation where communication between God and the individual is direct and straightforward.

As Pantheism has no central core of doctrine or dogmatic beliefs, since it relies on rational propositions, there is an enormous sense of tolerance for the variety of religions in the world. Religions usually clash on points of doctrine. One faith believes very firmly that something is true, and a different faith believes in perhaps a contrary model for the world and for God. As these beliefs are often points of accepted faith, there is usually very little room for manoeuvre. Ultimately one has to accept that one belief system is correct and the other is incorrect. Pantheism does not, however, have the need for doctrine, and hence there are few points of disagreement with other religions. Pantheism can accept other faiths while at the same time holding on to its own model of the universe.

On death, the human body disintegrates, and its organic elements disperse to aid future life. According to pantheists there is no afterlife or reincarnation, but we do live on in a sense. We live on through the effects of the acts which we have performed in this life, and through our achievements. We live in the collective memory of those who have known us. We also live on in the things we have taught others or said to others. We all influence those around us, and they in turn will influence the next generation. Our ideas continue after our death. There is a continuity from one generation to another. The ideas and thoughts which we have today are in part the products of those who have gone before.

As we peer over our shoulders, there stretching back through time are those who have passed this way before, and beyond us, reaching on to the horizon, are those who will tread this earth after we have gone. They will speak our ideas and voice our concerns, and look over their shoulders at us. We are all linked, and forever will be. That is the ultimate heart of mysticism.

KEY IDEAS

It is possible that mysticism is shared by all of humanity, and that there is a potential mystical experience which is accessible to all. However, different faiths may have their unique forms of mysticism which have evolved in part from the culture of that faith. Whichever is nearer the truth, the possibility of an experience which transcends ordinary existence, continues to inspire us.

GLOSSARY

Asana	A posture in Hatha yoga.
Ashlag, Yehuda	A famous kabbalistic teacher who died in Israel in 1954. He wrote a celebrated analysis of the Zohar, and became a rabbi at Jerusalem.
Ashram	A monastery within the Hindu tradition.
Cathars	A Christian mystical sect which developed in the south of France in the eleventh century. Regarded as heretical by the Catholic Church, the sect was defeated and destroyed by the Albigensian Crusade established by Pope Innocent III.
Chan Buddhism	The School of Buddhism in China which eventually developed into Zen.
Dhikr	Within Islam, the concentration of the mind upon God, by means of repeating the name of God.
Feng Shui	Within Taoism, the principle of orientating artefacts or buildings in harmony with the natural flow of energy or qi.
Fox, George	The founder of the Quaker movement or Religious Society of Friends.
Gurmukh	In Sikhism, a person who is devoted to the spiritual life.
Guru Nanak	The founder of the Sikh religion, who was born in the Panjab in 1469 CE.
Haiku	A short Japanese poem of 17 syllables, usually expressing the spiritual ideas of Zen.

Hasidism	An eighteenth-century movement within Judaism founded by the Baal Shem Tov. It advocates a direct devotion to God, and a sense of caring for other human beings.
Icon	Christian religious painting, particularly within the Eastern Orthodox Church.
Kabbalah	A body of knowledge representing the mystical tradition within Judaism.
Kami	Spirits worshipped within the religion of Shinto.
Koan	A verbal puzzle, often apparently irrational in nature, given to students in Rinzai Zen Buddhist training.
Kyudo	A form of archery in Japan, often employed as a type of spiritual discipline linked to Zen.
Luria, Isaac	A leading sixteenth-century teacher and philosopher of Kabbalah.
Mahakasyapa	The name of the Buddha's disciple who understood the Buddha's teaching when the latter held up a flower. This transmission of teaching was the beginning of the Zen movement.
Mahavira	The mystic and teacher who summarized the philosophy of Jainism, and helped to spread Jain teachings.
Mala	In Hinduism, the name of a set of beads used as an aid in the repetition of a mantra.
Mandala	A symmetrical, symbolic diagram used as an object of meditation in, for example, Tibetan Buddhism.
Matsuo Basho	A seventeenth-century Japanese poet, famous for his haiku poems.
Meister Eckhart	A fourteenth-century German philosopher, theologian and mystic.
Moksha	In Hinduism, the release of the individual soul from samsara, the cycle of birth

	and death. This provides the opportunity for the soul to merge with Brahman.
Monism	The idea that the universe is a single entity, and that it is impossible to distinguish any separate elements.
Monotheism	The doctrine that there is a single God.
Mul Mantra	The statement at the beginning of the Sikh scripture, the Guru Granth Sahib.
Nam Simran	Within Sikhism, the remembrance of the name of God.
Panentheism	The doctrine that God is present everywhere, but that God is more important than the rest of the Universe. God is considered to be transcendent and all-powerful.
Pantheism	The doctrine that God is present throughout the universe. God is seen as being part of everything in the universe, and everything is also an element of God.
Pranayama	Breathing exercises within yoga.
Puja	A Hindu religious ceremony.
Quietists	A seventeenth-century spiritual movement in Europe, which through devotional practices aimed to develop a close, personal relationship with God.
Sadhu	A wandering Hindu mystic.
Sahaj	In Sikhism, the state of mystical union with God.
Satori	The state of enlightenment in Zen Buddhism.
Sefer Yetzirah	A kabbalistic text said to contain revelations to Abraham.
Sephirot	Within kabbalistic tradition, the concept of God in ten aspects which are important in the Creation process. God is perceived as using these aspects for the improvement of human existence.

Shaolin monastery	A monastery in Hunan province in China, reputed to be the place where Kung Fu was first developed.
Shaykh	A spiritual teacher within the Sufi tradition.
Syncretism	The combining together of several beliefs from different religions.
Talmud	The compilation of the Jewish Oral Law, consisting of interpretations of the Torah.
Tao	The spiritual force behind the universe, ensuring that all elements of the universe are in harmony.
Tao Te Ching	The principal scripture of Taoism, assumed to be written by Laozi.
Tariqah	A religious order within Sufism.
Thanka	A Tibetan Buddhist religious painting, which may be used as the object of meditation.
Theosophical Society	A new religious movement founded in 1875. It is monistic in nature and influenced by Hinduism.
Tirthankaras	In Jainism, the historical sages who have helped others to achieve enlightenment.
Torah	The first five books of the Jewish Bible, often termed the Pentateuch. The Torah is considered to have been revealed by God to Moses on Mount Sinai.
Vajrayana	The School of Mahayana Buddhism, typical of Tibet.
Weil, Simone	Twentieth-century French philosopher, religious thinker, mystic and social reformer.
Wu wei.	In Taoism, the philosophy of acting within the harmony of the Tao, without there being any obvious signs of action.
Zazen	Meditation practice within Zen Buddhism.

Zohar   Kabbalistic text which is an analysis of, and commentary upon, the first five books of the Hebrew Bible. It also contains a discussion of the nature of the human soul and of ethics.

BIBLIOGRAPHY

Alston, W. P. (2005) 'Mysticism and Perceptual Awareness of God', in Mann, W. E. ed. *The Blackwell Guide to the Philosophy of Religion.* Oxford: Blackwell.

Armstrong, K. (2000) *Buddha.* London: Phoenix.

Avari, B. (2007) *India: The Ancient Past.* London: Routledge.

Baldick, J. (2000) *Mystical Islam: An Introduction to Sufism.* London: Tauris Parke.

Chah, A. (2005) *Everything Arises, Everything Falls Away* (trans. P. Breiter). London: Shambhala.

Charlesworth, M. (2002) *Philosophy and Religion: from Plato to Postmodernism.* Oxford: OneWorld.

Chittick, W. C. (2000) *Sufism: A Short Introduction.* Oxford: OneWorld.

Chryssides, G. D. and Geaves, R. (2007) *The Study of Religion: An Introduction to Key Ideas and Methods.* London: Continuum.

Clarke, J. J. (2000) *The Tao of the West: Western transformations of Taoist Thought.* London: Routledge.

Cohn-Sherbok, L. and D. (1997) *Judaism: A Short Introduction.* Oxford: OneWorld.

Cole, P. (2004) *Philosophy of Religion*, 2nd edn. London: Hodder and Stoughton.

Cole, P. (2005) *Religious Experience.* London: Hodder Murray.

Coleman, G. and Jinpa, T. eds. (2005) *The Tibetan Book of the Dead or The Great Liberation by Hearing in the Intermediate States.* London: Penguin.

De Lange, N. (2003) *Judaism.* Oxford: Oxford University Press.

Easwaran, E. (1975) *The Bhagavad Gita for Daily Living.* Berkeley: Blue Mountain Centre.

Flood, G. (1999) *Beyond Phenomenology: Rethinking the Study of Religion.* London: Continuum.

Geaves, R. (2006) *Key Words in Religious Studies.* London: Continuum.

Gouvion, C. and Jouvion, P. (1993) *The Gardeners of God: An Encounter with Five Million Baha'is.* Oxford: OneWorld.

Harvey, G. (2005) *Animism: Respecting the Living World.* London: Hurst.

Ingle, L. H. (1994) *First Among Friends: George Fox and the Creation of Quakerism.* Oxford: Oxford University Press.

Isshu, M. and Sasaki, R. F. (1993) *The Zen Koan.* New York: Harcourt Brace.

King, U. (1980) *Towards a New Mysticism: Teilhard de Chardin and Eastern Religions.* London: Collins.

Knysh, A. (2000) *Islamic Mysticism: A Short History.* Leiden: E. J. Brill.
Kohn, L. and LaFargue, M. eds. (1998) *Lao-Tzu and the Tao-Te-Ching.* New York: State University of New York Press.
Kripal, J. J. (2006) 'Mysticism', in Segal, R. A. ed. *The Blackwell Companion to the Study of Religion.* Oxford: Blackwell.
Lambert, M. (1998) *The Cathars.* Oxford: Blackwell.
Leaman, O. (2006) *Jewish Thought: An introduction.* London: Routledge.
Littleton, C. S. (2002) *Shinto: Origins, Rituals, Festivals, Spirits, Sacred Places.* Oxford: Oxford University Press.
Mackenzie, V. (1998) *Cave in the Snow.* London: Bloomsbury.
McLellan, D. (1990) *Utopian Pessimist: The Life and Thought of Simone Weil.* New York: Poseidon.
Maezumi, T. (2002) *Appreciate Your Life: The Essence of Zen Practice.* London: Shambhala.
Matthiessen, P. (1979) *The Snow Leopard.* London: Picador.
Michaels, A. (2004) *Hinduism: Past and Present.* Princeton: Princeton University Press.
Momen, M. (1997) *The Baha'i Faith.* Oxford: OneWorld.
Parrinder, G. (1995) *Mysticism in the World's Religions.* Oxford: OneWorld.
Rosen, J. (2003) *Understanding Judaism.* Edinburgh: Dunedin.
Roy, A. K. (1984) *A History of the Jains.* New Delhi: Gitanjali.
Schimmel, A. (1978) *The Triumphal Sun: A Study of the Works of Jalaloddin Rumi.* London: East-West.
Shackle, C. and Singh, A. P. (2005) *Teachings of the Sikh Gurus.* London: Routledge.
Sheldrake, P. (2007) *A Brief History of Spirituality.* Oxford: Blackwell
Shokek, S. (2001) *Kabbalah and the Art of Being.* London: Routledge.
Singh, K. (2005) *A History of the Sikhs.* Oxford: Oxford University Press.
Smart, N. (1999) *World Philosophies.* London: Routledge.
Suzuki, D. T. (2004) *The Training of the Zen Buddhist Monk.* Tokyo: Cosimo.
Tobin, F. (1986) *Meister Eckhart: Thought and Language.* Philadelphia: University of Pennsylvania Press.
Trimingham, J. S. (1971) *The Sufi Orders in Islam.* Oxford: Oxford University Press.
Underhill, E. (1999) *The Essentials of Mysticism.* Oxford: OneWorld.
Vaudeville, C. (1998) *A Weaver Named Kabir.* New York: Oxford University Press.
Watts, A. (1975) *Tao: The Watercourse Way.* New York: Pantheon.
Watts, A. (2000) *What is Zen?* Novato: New World Library.
Yeshe, L. T. (1987) *Introduction to Tantra: The Transformation of Desire.* Boston: Wisdom.

FURTHER READING

Aranya, Swami H. (1983) *Yoga Philosophy of Patanjali.* Albany: State University of New York Press.

Baldick, J. (1989) *Mystical Islam: An Introduction to Sufism.* London: I. B. Tauris.

Bell, R. H. ed. (1993) *Simone Weil's Philosophy of Culture: Readings towards a Divine Humanity.* Cambridge: Cambridge University Press.

Bhattacharya, N. N. (1999) *History of the Tantric Religion.* New Delhi: Manohar.

Bowker, J. W. (2002) *The Cambridge Illustrated History of Religions.* Cambridge: Cambridge University Press.

Davidson, R. M. (2005) *Tibetan Renaissance: Tantric Buddhism in the Rebirth of Tibetan Culture.* New York: Columbia University Press.

Ernst, C. W. (1985) *Words of Ecstasy in Sufism.* Albany: State University of New York Press.

Ferguson, A. (2000) *Zen's Chinese Heritage.* Boston: Wisdom.

Feuerstein, G. (1989) *Yoga: The Technology of Ecstasy.* Wellingborough: Crucible.

Flood, G. (1996) *An Introduction to Hinduism.* Cambridge: Cambridge University Press.

Ghose, A. (1971) *Synthesis of Yoga.* Pondicherry: Sri Aurobindo Ashram.

Glick, L. (1999) *Abraham's Heirs: Jews and Christians in Medieval Europe.* Syracuse: Syracuse University Press.

Gyatso, G. K. (2003) *Tantric Grounds and Paths.* Glen Spey: Tharpa.

Hallamish, M. (1999) *An Introduction to the Kabbalah.* Albany: State University of New York Press.

Harper, K. A. and Brown, R. L. (2002) *The Roots of Tantra.* Albany: State University of New York Press.

Hoffman, V. J. (1995) *Sufism, Mystics and Saints in Modern Egypt.* Columbia: University of South Caroline Press.

Kirkland, R. (2004) *Taoism: The Enduring Tradition.* London: Routledge.

Klostermaier, K. (1994) *A Survey of Hinduism.* Albany: State University of New York Press.

Kohn, L. (1993) *The Taoist Experience: An Anthology.* Albany: State University of New York Press.

Merton, T. (1967) *Mystics and Zen Masters.* New York: Farrar, Strauss and Giroux.

Miller, J. (2003) *Daoism: A Short Introduction.* Oxford: OneWorld.

Nicholson, R. A. (1978) *Studies in Islamic Mysticism.* Cambridge: Cambridge University Press.

Quinn, P. (2005) *Philosophy of Religion A–Z.* Edinburgh: Edinburgh University Press.

Ray, R. A. (2001) *Secret of the Vajra World: The Tantric Buddhism of Tibet.* Boston: Shambhala.

Schipper, K. and Franciscus, V. (2004) *The Taoist Canon: A Historical Companion to the Daozang.* Chicago: University of Chicago Press.

Segal, R. (2004) *Myth: A Very Short Introduction.* Oxford: Oxford University Press.

Shah, I. (1980) *The Way of the Sufi.* London: Octagon.

Zaehner, R. C. (1969) *The Bhagavad Gita.* Oxford: Oxford University Press.

INDEX